THE WORLD SERIES

THE GREAT CONTESTS

BY
RICHARD J. BRENNER

EAST END PUBLISHING

With great love and affection to my children, Halle and Jason,
to my wife, Anita, and to my mother, Betty,
Thank you for your belief in me and your encouragement.
To Ms. Catherine Lynch, a rare teacher and spirit,
and to Malcolm Largman, another special teacher
and the first person who ever encouraged me to write—
to both of you, from a long time ago,
I've never forgotten either of you.

The author wishes to acknowledge the following:
The *New York Times*
Newsday
The World Series: A 75th Anniversary
edited by Joseph L. Reichler

Text Copyright © 1987 1988 1989 by Richard J. Brenner
Library of Congress Catalog Card Number: 87-15553
ISBN: 0-943403-00-6

—Cover Photo: Michael Zagaris

Library of Congress Cataloging-in-Publication Data
Brenner, Richard J., 1941-
    The World Series.

    Summary: Recounts memorable World Series contests,
including the 1955 series between the Brooklyn Dodgers and
the New York Yankees, the 1975 series between the
Cincinnati Reds and the Boston Red Sox, and the 1986
series between the New York Mets and the Boston Red Sox.
    1. World series (Baseball)—History—Juvenile
literature. [1. World series (Baseball) 2. Baseball—
History] I. Title.
GV863.A1B74   1987   796.357'782   87-15553
ISBN 0-943403-00-6

Printed in the United States of America.

Introduction

The groundwork for what would come to be known as the World Series was laid in 1882 when Cincinnati, the top team in the American Association (the American League had not yet been formed), challenged Chicago of the National League to a championship series. But the players fought and argued so much that the teams just called it quits after they had played only a few games. From 1884–1890, the top teams in the two leagues played each other, but there were no set plans or number of games—one year they would play 3 games and another year, 15. Then they finally just stopped playing.

The first real World Series took place in 1903. It came about because the owner of the Pittsburgh Pirates, the National League champs, challenged the American League champs, the Boston Pilgrims (who would later be called the Red Sox), to a play-off series. The N.L. had been in existence for 28 years and wanted to put the upstart A.L., which was only three years old, in its place. But Boston, behind the pitching of Bill Dinneen (three victories, including two shutouts) and Cy Young (who would retire as the winningest pitcher in baseball with 511 victories), defeated the Pirates five games to three. (The leagues didn't finally settle on a best-of-seven format until 1922.)

The World Series wasn't played in 1904 because the owner and manager of the New York Giants refused to play a team from "the minor league". The outcry from fans was so strong, though, that the Series was resumed in 1905 and has been played every year since then.

The 1905 World Series was one of the most remarkable of all time. The Giants, who were again tops in the N.L., defeated the Philadelphia Athletics, 4-1. Each of the five victories were shutouts and three of the five were pitched by one man, Christy Mathewson! (Matty would go on to record 373 regular season wins and become one of the five original members of the Hall of Fame.)

In 1906, George Rohe helped the White Sox to one of the biggest upsets in a World Series. The White Sox, who hit so badly (their team average was a microscopic .230) that they were called the "hitless wonders", defeated the mighty Cubs, who had won 116 games during the season (still the record for most games won in a season), four games to two. George Rohe wasn't a very good ballplayer. He only played in the majors for three years (1905-1907) and only managed to hit .212, .258, and .213. And Rohe only got to play in the World Series because another player was injured. But for a brief, shining moment in time, George Rohe was a star as he batted .333 during the World Series. His triple in the first game led to a 2-1 victory and in game three, he hit another triple, which knocked in all the runs in a 3-0 win.

The Detroit Tigers, led by the great Ty Cobb, played in and lost the World Series in 1907, 1908, and 1909. Cobb is considered by many people to be the greatest player ever to wear spikes. He played in the majors for 24 seasons and, except for the first one, batted over .300 every year. He batted over .400 three times and when he retired, his career batting average was an astonishing .367, the highest career batting average of all time. But when it came to the World Series, Cobb managed to hit over .300 just once (in 1908), while batting .200 in 1907 and .231 in 1909.

Those first few contests show why the World Series has always delighted baseball fans: the clash of great teams; the thrill of watching the underdog upset the favorite; the drama of watching great stars shine (like Mathewson), or flicker (like Cobb); and the excitement of seeing little-known ballplayers with small talents (like George Rohe) briefly blaze like a shooting star across the baseball skies.

Through the years, the "Fall Classic" has provided millions of people the thrill of viewing this great sporting spectacle and sharing in its magic moments: watch ing Babe Ruth point to the centerfield seats in the 1932 Series and then, seeing him hit a home run right to where he had pointed; or watching Enos Slaughter race home from first base on a single to give the 1946 Cardinals the winning run in the seventh game. No one who saw the 1956 World Series will ever forget the fifth game when Yankee pitcher Don Larsen pitched the only perfect game in the history of the World Series. And no one who watched will ever forget the 1969 Series in which the "Miracle Mets", a team that had been picked for last place, beat the Baltimore Orioles.

Now we will take a close look at some of the most exciting World Series of all time—we hope that you enjoy the view.

CHAPTER 1

This Is Next Year!

In 1955, the world was, in many ways, not too different from the way it is today. Newspaper headlines, then and now, spoke about trouble in the Middle East, crime, and the need for nuclear disarmament.

In other ways, however, the world was very different from today. In the area of sports, for instance, the National Football League had only 12 teams, which were divided into Eastern and Western conferences. The AFC didn't exist and neither did the Super Bowl.

In baseball, the National and American leagues each had only eight teams, and the teams that were in first place at the end of the season played each other in the World Series. (Play-offs only happened on those rare occasions when two teams were tied at the end of the season.) Most regular-season games and all World Series games were played during the day and all the games were played on real grass; there wasn't any artificial turf.

For millions of people, though, the main way that the world is different now is that in 1955 the Dodgers played in Brooklyn, where they belonged, and not in Los Angeles.

Brooklyn is one of the five boroughs that make up the City of New York. Because it is so large and heavily populated, if Brooklyn had been a city, it would have been the fourth-largest city in America. But Brooklyn was divided up into neighborhoods—with names like Flatbush and Bensonhurst and Bay Ridge—that gave the people living in these areas the feeling that they were living in a small town.

The relationship between the people of Brooklyn and the Dodgers was a very special one that lasted through good times and bad times (as when the Dodgers finished in either sixth or seventh place 12 times in 17 seasons between 1922 and 1938). And even in the good times, there was always a letdown because the Dodgers were never able to win a World Series. Seven times they had tried and seven times they had lost. The last five times—1941, 1947, 1949, 1952, and 1953—they had lost to one team: the New York Yankees.

The Yankees were the undisputed lords of baseball. Their history rang with names like Babe Ruth, Lou Gehrig, and Joe DiMaggio. And between 1921, when they played in their first World Series, and 1953, 33 World Series had been played. Incredibly, the Yankees had played in 20 of them, winning 16 (6 of them in four-game sweeps)! Almost unbelievably, they had won 5 straight World Series between 1949 and 1953, and after a year's absence in 1954, they were hungry and back for more in 1955.

And what made all of this worse for Dodger fans was that the Yankees played just a subway ride away in the Bronx, another of New York City's boroughs. The Giants, the National League rivals of the Dodgers, played in the Polo Grounds, which was also just a subway ride from Ebbets Field, home of the Brooklyn Dodgers. So every year, Dodger fans had to suffer the taunts of people they worked with and went to school with. Sometimes a person even had Giant and Yankee fans in his own family!

But the Flatbush Faithful, as the Brooklyn fans were sometimes called, never lost their love or their faith in their team. And every year, the cry would ring out through the streets of Brooklyn from Coney Island to Bedford Avenue, "Wait until next year!"

Nineteen fifty-five looked as if it might really be "next year"—the year that Brooklyn finally won a World Series. They had gotten off to a great start by winning their first 10 games of the regular season and quickly building a big lead. They had finished a comfortable 13½ games ahead of the second-place Milwaukee (now Atlanta) Braves.

They had an outstanding line-up that was anchored by future Hall-of-Famer Roy Campanella behind the plate. Campy, who was a great catcher, was also a ferocious hitter, who had hit .318 with 32 homers while driving in 107 runs during the regular season. He was also a team leader and one of the nicest men in the world. At first base was Gil Hodges, who hit 27 homers and had 102 RBI's. Many people consider him to be the finest fielding first baseman of all time. Second base was divided between Don Zimmer and Jim Gilliam, a switch-hitter. Shortstop belonged to Pee Wee Reese, the clutch-hitting, smooth-fielding captain of the Dodgers, who was also destined for the Hall of Fame. At third base was an exceptional man as well as an exceptional athlete—Jackie Robinson. Jackie, who had been an All-American running back in college and a star basketball player as well, was the first black man to be allowed to play in the major leagues. His ability, his character, and his courage set standards for everyone, both black and white. But he was nearly 37 years old now and time had robbed him of the skills that had earned him the Rookie of the Year Award in 1947 and the Most Valuable Player award in 1949. However, he still had his fierce pride and determination, and at critical times he could still win a ballgame with his bat, his glove, his legs, his head, or his courage. He also later earned election to the Hall of Fame.

Left field was shared by Gilliam—when he wasn't at second base—and a short, speedy Cuban named Sandy Amoros, who could hit for average and power. Center field was the property of another future Hall of Famer, Edwin "Duke" Snider. He was a spectacular fielder, had great speed, and was a super hitter. In 1955, he batted .309 while socking 42 homers and knocking in 136 runs. Right field was patrolled by Carl Furillo, an excellent outfielder with an exceptionally strong arm who had batted .314 with 26 homers and 95 RBI's.

The big question mark for the Dodgers was their pitching staff. Don Newcombe had gotten off to a fantastic start and had a 17-1 record in July. But he tailed off after that and was able to win only three games the rest of the season. Most of the other starting pitchers had also pitched poorly in the second half of the season. The Brooklyn front office turned to their minor leagues for help and came up with rookies Don Bessent and Roger Craig. Some of the Dodgers, like Johnny Podres, who had a 9-10 record, suffered from sore arms. Podres had also lost a decision to a metal batting cage near the end of the season and almost wasn't kept on the roster for the World Series. The only reliable exception to Brooklyn's pitching problems was Clem Labine, a tough right-hander with a wicked sinker who was used mostly as a relief pitcher.

The Yankees did not have it so easy in the American League. They were in a three-way fight for the pennant for most of the season with the Chicago White Sox and the Cleveland Indians. As late as September 13, the Yanks were two and one-half games back, but an eight-game winning streak put them into first place and they held on to win by a slim margin.

The Yankees also had a future Hall of Fame

catcher anchoring their team; his name was Lawrence "Yogi" Berra. He had hit .272 with 27 homers and 108 RBI's, and acted as a coach on the field for the Yankees. The Yankees used a platoon system at first base with lefty Joe Collins playing against right-handed pitching and righty Bill "Moose" Skowron playing against left-handed pitchers. Together they had combined for 25 home runs and 106 RBI's. The second baseman was Billy Martin, the hero of the Yanks' 1953 World Series victory over the Dodgers. Martin would go on to become manager of the Yankees, and other teams, too. Shortstop was shared by Phil Rizzuto and Jerry Coleman—terrific fielders and adequate hitters. Third base was handled by the steady Gil McDougald.

The outfield was solid with Irv Noren in left, the great Mickey Mantle in center, and the clutch-hitting, hard-throwing Hank Bauer in right. Mantle had had an outstanding season with a .309 average, 37 homers, 99 RBI's, but he had torn a muscle in his thigh two weeks before the Series was to begin and it was uncertain if he could play. The Yankees had strong reserves but all of them put together wouldn't make up for the absence of Mantle. The Yankees had a solid pitching staff led by Whitey Ford, Tommy Byrne, and Bob Turley. The manager of the Yankees was Casey Stengel, the man whom many people consider to be the greatest manager of all time. Even if Mantle couldn't play, most experts figured that either Stengel would find a way for the Yankees to win or

Brooklyn would find a way to lose.

The weather was overcast the morning of the first game, and although the sky cleared before noon, the 63,000 fans who filled Yankee Stadium saw the Yanks drop a little more rain on Dodger dreams.

The Dodgers did manage to jump out to an early lead against Yankee ace Whitey Ford in the second inning, as Carl Furillo hit a midget home run to right field that just hit the top of the low railing and bounced into the seats. Jackie Robinson followed with a tremendous drive to left center that measured more than 400 feet and he raced to third with a triple. Don Zimmer blooped a single over the infield and the Dodgers led, 2-0.

But the Yankees, like some jealous Greek gods, tied the game in the bottom of the inning on a two-run home run off Don Newcombe by rookie left fielder Elston Howard. Howard, who was playing while Mantle continued to nurse his injury, became one of the few players to hit a home run in his first at-bat in a World Series.

The Dodgers took the lead again in the top of the third when Duke Snider hit a tremendous blast into the right-field stands. But the Yanks tied it in their next turn at bat on a walk, a single, and two groundouts. In the fourth, Joe Collins hit a homer to give the Yanks a 4-3 lead, and in the sixth, he followed a single by Yogi Berra with another homer and the Yanks led, 6-3. One out later, Billy Martin lined a triple over Gilliam's head in left field and Walter Alston, the

Dodger manager, decided that Newcombe had pitched long enough. He brought in Don Bessent, a rookie right-hander and Casey Stengel responded by putting in a left-handed pinch hitter, Eddie Robinson, for Rizzuto. But Robinson never got to swing the bat because after he took a pitch for a ball and Bessent went into his windup for the next pitch, Martin took off in an attempt to steal home. Martin and the pitch arrived at almost the same instant but a quick tag by Campy was just in time to get Martin and retire the Yanks.

Furillo opened the eighth inning with a single for his third straight hit. Hodges flied out and Jackie Robinson hit a sharp grounder to third base for what should have been an easy out, maybe a double play, but Gil McDougald let the ball get by him and Furillo made it to third and Robinson to second. Zimmer then hit a sacrifice fly that scored Furillo and sent Robinson to third. Ford checked Robinson, who was dancing off third. As Whitey went into his windup, Jackie dashed for home. Ford delivered the pitch and Yogi made the tag, but this time the umpire yelled "safe". Berra argued the call but, as always, the umpire won the argument. It was the 18th time that Jackie had stolen home in his remarkable career, and only the 9th time that it had ever been accomplished in a World Series game. The Yanks' lead had been cut to 6-5.

The Dodgers came close in the ninth when, after Snider singled, Campy hit a wicked liner to deep right field. But it didn't have enough height and the Yanks won the opening game.

Although Mantle's injury didn't allow him to play, Joe Collins, who had hit two homers, told reporters that Mickey had helped the Yanks win. How? Because he had used Mickey's bat to swat the homers. "I'm going to keep right on using it. There's real good wood in that bat."

Walt Alston, the Dodger manager, assured everyone that the team was still confident and so was he. Campy, who always seemed to be able to manage a smile and find a silver lining behind any dark cloud, spoke about his long out in the ninth. "If I had just hit it a little higher instead of on a line, it would have been in the stands."

For the Brooklyn Dodgers, there always seemed to be an "if".

The Dodgers looked sharp in the beginning of the second game. Billy Loes shut the Yanks out for three innings and struck out five. He was especially tough in the second when, after Yogi had reached second, he struck out Collins, Howard, and Martin. And the Dodgers broke through for a run off Tommy Byrne in the fourth when Reese doubled and Snider singled him home.

The Yanks answered back in the bottom of the fourth when, with two out, Berra singled and Collins walked. Elston Howard singled for one run and Martin singled for a second. Eddie Robinson, pinch hitting for Rizzuto, was hit by a pitch and Tommy Byrne, the Yankee pitcher, hit a two-run single. The Dodgers managed to hold the Yanks the rest of the way and come up with a run in the fifth, but it was too late. Tommy Byrne pitched a five-hitter and the Yanks had won again, 4-2.

The victory was especially sweet for the 35-year-old Tommy Bryne because he had had to work hard and struggle his way back to the majors after spending a year in the minors learning how to become an effective pitcher.

The Dodgers had battered southpaws (left-handers) all year. In fact, only one left-hander had pitched a complete game against them and he had lost. Now within 24 hours, they had lost to two lefties and had managed, naturally, to do it in the World Series.

After the game, Pee Wee Reese, talking about Billy Loes, said, "The way he was going, I thought he would shut them out. I thought this was going to be Billy's day."

But it wasn't Billy's day and it wasn't the Dodger's day. They were down two games to none and no team had ever been down 2-0 in a 4-of-7 Series and come back to win it!

For the third game, the scene shifted to cozy Ebbets Field, the home of the Brooklyn Dodgers. "Bullet" Bob Turley, a fast-balling right-hander who had had a 17-13 record, opened for the Yankees. To the delight of the Flatbush Faithful, the Dodgers jumped out to a 2-0 lead in the first when Campy smacked a two-out homer after Pee Wee had walked.

But the Yanks went on the attack in the second as Mantle, despite the fact he was playing in pain, smashed a homer into the center-field stands off Dodger starter Johnny Podres. Bill "Moose" Skowron, playing first base against the left-handed Podres, doubled to left. Podres retired the next two hitters, but Rizzuto singled to left. Skowron was running all the way with two out but a fine throw by Sandy Amoros got the ball to Campy in plenty of time. But Skowron, who had played college football at Purdue, barreled into Campy and the sure-handed catcher dropped the ball as Skowron scored the tying run. The Dodgers had lost the lead again; they could not afford to lose another game.

Brooklyn responded by bouncing back in their half of the second. Robinson singled, Amoros walked, and Podres bunted so well while attempting to sacrifice that he beat the throw. Turley walked Gilliam to force in a run and Casey Stengel walked out to the mound to remove Turley. Tom Morgan, the new pitcher, walked Pee Wee to force in another run before retiring the side. Brooklyn upped their lead to 6-2 in the fourth as Gilliam singled, Duke walked, Campy singled in Gilliam—moving Duke to third—and Furillo hit a long foul fly to left, allowing Duke to tag up and score.

The Yanks threatened in the sixth when Mantle came up to hit after McDougald and Berra had singled. The Flatbush Faithful grew tense but Podres got Mantle to ground into a double play. The Yanks scored their last run of the day on a walk to Rizzuto and a pinch triple by Andy Carey. But the Dodgers answered with two more runs in the bottom of the seventh, which was started off by some great base running by Jackie Robinson. He lined a ball into the left-field corner and cruised around second base. Elston Howard wound up to fire the ball into second and as soon as he did, Jackie put on the afterburners and slid into third.

The Dodgers, with their 8-3 victory, had cut the Yanks' lead to 2-1 and Johnny Podres, who turned 23 that day, laughed, "This was the best birthday present I ever had."

In game four, the Yanks jumped out to a quick lead on a Gil McDougald homer off Carl Erskine in the first inning. They added another run in the second on an RBI single by Rizzuto. The Dodgers cut the lead to 2-1 on a single by Amoros and a two-bagger by Gilliam but the Yanks upped it to 3-1 on an RBI single by Billy Martin in the top of the fourth.

In the bottom of the fourth, the Brooklyn bats began to boom. Campy homered to left off Don Larsen, and after Furillo beat out an infield roller, Gil Hodges hit a huge homer over the scoreboard in right center to give the Dodgers a 4-3 lead.

The crowd in Ebbets Field was roaring, and the roars grew louder when Clem Labine, the Dodgers' relief ace, came in to snuff out a fifth-inning threat. In the bottom of the fifth, Larsen walked Gilliam, and after he threw two balls to Pee Wee, Stengel replaced him with Johnny Kucks. Pee Wee beat out an infield bouncer after Gilliam had stole second. Duke Snider strolled to the plate, jumped on a pitch, and sent it sailing high and far over the right-field screen and across Bedford Avenue to give the Dodgers a 7-3 lead. The fans went wild!

But they grew hushed in the sixth when the Yanks pushed across two quick runs as Howard singled, Martin doubled him home, and pinch hitter Eddie Robinson doubled home Martin. Only a great catch by Snider in center field prevented more scoring.

The Dodgers, though, picked up another run in the seventh and Labine pitched no-hit ball for the final three innings, so the Dodgers won 8-5 and evened the series at 2-2. They had climbed up and out of the hole they had been in but they hadn't impressed the Yanks. Berra said that Labine had been "lucky" and Phil "The Scooter" Rizzuto said, "We'll win the Series. Maybe it will go seven games, but we'll win it."

But Brooklyn had other ideas. In the second inning of game five, after Hodges singled, Amoros drilled a homer over the screen in right off Bob Grim. In the third, Snider continued to punish Yankee pitching with a solo blast over the screen, and the Dodgers led 3-0 behind rookie Roger Craig's pitching. They might have gotten more, too, but Irv Noren, playing center for Mantle (who had aggravated his injury) made an excellent catch. The Yanks did break through with a run in the fourth though when the pesky Martin singled in Berra. The Dodgers scored again in the fifth with a towering home run way over the screen in right by—who else?—Duke Snider. It was his fourth homer of the series and he became the only player ever to hit four home runs in more than one World Series (he had also done it in 1952).

The Yanks stormed back with a solo homer by pinch hitter Bob Cerv in the seventh off Roger Craig and another by Yogi in the eighth off Clem Labine. Labine avoided more trouble by getting Martin to ground into a double play. After an RBI single by Jackie Robinson in the bottom of the eighth, Labine knocked off the Yanks one-two-three in the ninth for a 5-3 Brooklyn win, and the Dodgers led the Series, 3-2.

In the clubhouse after the game, an excited Jackie Robinson was shouting happily "Four straight, four straight." And, even the usually quiet Gil Hodges told reporters, "If you think we went after them at Ebbets Field, wait until tomorrow at the Stadium. We'll swarm all over them like a pack of tigers."

But it was the Yankees who wound up devouring the Dodgers. The Yankees scored five runs in the first inning off lefty Karl Spooner, helped by two fielding mistakes by Gilliam, and a three-run homer by Moose Skowron that just made it into the lower right-field stands. And in the third, Snider injured his knee and had to leave the game when he stepped into a hole while chasing a fly ball. No one knew if he would be ready for game seven if the Dodgers lost game six.

The Dodgers scored a meaningless run in the fourth and mounted a couple of threats later in the game but they were turned back by the pitching of

Whitey Ford (who gave up only four hits while striking out eight for his second victory in the Series) and a marvelous fielding play in the seventh inning by Joe Collins, who had replaced Skowron at first base in the fifth.

Casey Stengel and the Yankee players were confident about the seventh game. Tommy Byrne, who had baffled the Dodgers in the second game, was all ready, and after all, the Yankees almost always won and the Dodgers never had.

The weather was sunny on Tuesday, October 4, as 62,455 people filled Yankee Stadium for the seventh and final game. Baseball fans all across the city huddled around TV sets or turned on their radios. People who had to go out walked through the streets with portable radios close to their ears. Snider could play, but Jackie Robinson was out with an injured foot. The umpire yelled, "Play ball." The game began.

Although the Yankees threatened in the second and third, the game remained scoreless until the fourth inning when Campy doubled to left and Gil Hodges brought him home with a two-out single off Byrne. Berra doubled to lead off the Yankee fourth but Podres retired the next three batters as the tension mounted. The Dodgers eked out another run in the sixth when Pee Wee, who had begun the inning with a single, eventually came in to score on a sacrifice fly by Hodges off Bob Grim who had relieved Byrne. The last out of the inning was made by George Shuba, who pinch-hit for Don Zimmer. That meant that Gilliam would move to second base and Sandy Amoros would come in to play left field.

Podres began the bottom of the sixth by walking Martin, and McDougald followed with a bunt single. The next batter was Yogi Berra, the Yankee clean-up hitter. One swing and the Dodgers' dream could be demolished. The Dodgers' outfield played Yogi deep and around to right to guard against his left-hand power.

Podres checked the runners and delivered a pitch on the outside part of the plate. Yogi swung and hit a fly ball down the left-field line. He hadn't pulled the ball, he had hit it to the opposite field, and Amoros was way out of position. As Sandy desperately raced across the outfield grass, Martin headed for third and McDougald rounded second. As the ball came out of the blue sky, Sandy, still running at full speed, stuck out his glove as far as he could and caught the ball! Then in one motion, he turned and fired the ball to Pee Wee, who relayed it to Hodges at first to double up McDougald. Amoros, who had just entered the game, had taken a game-tying hit away from Berra and turned it into a double play!

In the eighth, the Yanks erupted again when Rizzuto and McDougald singled. But Podres got Berra on a shallow fly to right and fanned the dangerous Hank Bauer.

All across the city, people stopped what they were doing to watch or listen to whether the Dodgers could hold their 2-0 lead in the ninth inning. Dodger fans, used to sudden disaster, held their breath. Skowron grounded to Podres for the first out and Cerv flied to left for the second out. Elston Howard came up to hit and time seemed to stop as Podres looked in for the sign and then the pitch was there and Howard hit a routine grounder to short. Pee Wee picked it up and threw it to Hodges at first for the final out of the 1955 World Series.

On the field, the Dodgers jumped and yelled for joy while all across Brooklyn, the noise of thousands of celebrating fans filled the air. People came out into the streets to shout their joy and share it with friends, neighbors, and total strangers. Pots were banged and caravans of cars with horns blasting moved along Flatbush Avenue and Ocean Parkway to announce that the wait was over.

NEXT YEAR WAS NOW!

CHAPTER 2

A Long Time Coming

The Pittsburgh Pirates and Cincinnati Reds were the dominant teams in the National League. The Pirates were about to represent the Eastern Division for the fifth time since 1970, while the Reds would be representing the Western Division for the fourth time since 1970.

The Pirates were out for revenge because they had lost to the Reds in the play-offs in 1970 and 1972. The Reds were on a mission of their own. They wanted to do what the Pirates had done in 1971. They wanted to win the 1975 World Series.

The Pirates had taken the Eastern Division by a six-and-one-half-game margin over the Phillies, mainly on the hitting of a group of sluggers led by Dave Parker with a .305 average, 25 homers, and 101 RBI's. He had plenty of support, too, from players like Willie Stargell (.292, 22, 90); Al Oliver (.280, 18,84); Richie Zisk (.290, 20, 75); Rennie Stennett, a hard-hitting second baseman (during the season, he became only the second player in baseball history to get seven hits in a game); and Manny Sanguillen, an excellent defensive catcher who also managed to hit .328.

The Reds started slowly during the regular season, but after manager Sparky Anderson moved all-star Pete Rose from left field to third base to make room in the line-up for George Foster's big bat, "the Big Red Machine" went into overdrive and won the Western Division title by a whopping 20 games. In one awesome stretch, they won 41 of 50 games!

The Reds seemed to have an all-star at every position, starting with Pete Rose, who had hit .317, marking the 10th time in 11 years that he had hit .300 or better. Behind the plate was the great Johnny Bench, the best catcher in baseball, who had hit .283 while smacking 28 homers and driving in 110 runs. At first base was Tony Perez (.282, 20, 109); Foster added punch in left with a .300 average and 23 homers; and Ken Griffey in right had hit .305. Dave Concepcion at short and Cesar Geronimo in center provided spectacular defense and respectable offense. The player who provided the spark that revved up the engine of the Big Red Machine, however, was second baseman Joe Morgan. At 5'7" and 155 pounds, Joe was small in size but large in ability. He had led the Reds in hitting with a .327 average while hitting 17 homers, driving in 94 runs, and scoring 107 himself. He also stole 68 bases in 78 attempts.

The Reds also had a solid group of starting pitchers headed by lefty Don Gullet, who had a 15-4 record and a 2.42 ERA, despite missing two months with a broken thumb. Right-handers Jack Billingham and Gary Nolan had also won 15 games and lefty Fred Norman had a 12-4 record. The bullpen was anchored by Rawly Eastwick (22 saves, 2.60 ERA); Will McEnany (15 saves, 2.47 ERA); Clay Carroll; and Pedro Borbon. The Machine was oiled and gassed and ready to run.

Pittsburgh manager Danny Murtagh started his ace, Jerry Reuss, in the first game of the best-of-five series. Reuss had an 18-11 regular-season record with a 2.54 ERA and had beaten the Reds three times. Murtagh had decided to feed the Reds a steady diet of left-handers since they had shown weakness against southpaws with a regular-season record of only 26-22. The Pirates jumped out to an early 2-0 lead at Cincinnati's Riverfront Stadium but the Reds cut it to 2-1 on an RBI single by pitcher Don Gullett. Joe Morgan began a three-run Reds' rally in the third when he drew a base on balls and then swiped second and third base on consecutive pitches. Reuss, losing his concentration because of Morgan's antics, walked Bench, and Perez followed with a single to score Morgan. Griffey then hit a two-out double to score Bench and Perez. They wrapped up the game in the fifth with four more runs, the last two coming on Gullett's first major-league home run, and cruised to an 8-3 victory.

In game two, the Reds got all the runs they needed in the first inning off lefty Jim Rooker when Rose singled and Perez homered. The Reds ran wild on the bases, stealing an almost unbelievable seven bases (in seven tries!), led by Ken Griffey with three. Norman and Eastwick combined on a five-hitter as the Reds romped, 6-1.

As the "scene of the crime" shifted to Pittsburgh's Three Rivers Stadium for game three, Sparky Anderson reminded the Reds, "You've got to win three games, not just two. We've been annihilated by Pittsburgh before and they could take three in a row."

Rookie John Candelaria was pitching a spectacular game for the Pirates. He had struck out seven of the first nine Reds and had given up only one hit, a second-inning homer by Dave Concepcion. He held a 2-1 lead entering the eighth inning, though, thanks to a two-run homer by Al Oliver in the sixth. "Candy" struck out the first two batters in the eighth—Griffey and Cesar Geronimo—for his 13th and 14th strikeouts, which broke the play-off record of 13 that Tom Seaver had set against the Reds in 1973. But pinch-hitter Merv Rettenmund walked and then Pete Rose got the second hit off Candy, a towering home run over the left-field fence that gave the Reds a 3-2 lead.

The Pirates caught up in the ninth with two walks after two singles forced in a run. But the Reds scored two in the tenth, beginning with a surprise two-strike bunt by Griffey and ending with a double by Joe Morgan. Pedro Borbon retired the Pirates in order in the bottom of the tenth and the Big Red Machine was humming and on its way to the World Series.

The Oakland A's had been ruling supreme over

the Kingdom of Baseball. They had won five straight divisional titles and for the last three years, they had won the World Series. And now they were ready for more; they were ready for number four.

The A's had two top starting pitchers, southpaws Vida Blue (22-11) and Ken Holtzman (18-14). They had an excellent bullpen led by Rollie Fingers (24 saves and 10 wins) and supported by Paul Lindblad (9-1) and rookie Jim Todd (8-3).

They were solid on defense and had a strong offense led by left fielder Claudell Washington, first baseman Joe Rudi, and "Mr. October" himself, Reggie Jackson. (Reggie is called Mr. October because of his excellent performance during the month of October, the month of play-off and World Series games). During the season, he had tied for the league lead with 36 homers.

The A's had taken an early lead in their division and, after April 28, had held first place for all but two days. They wound up coasting in to a seven-game lead over second-place Kansas City and they had such an easy time and played with such confidence that Reggie said, "We only played five games where we were nervous and excited and afraid to lose: three against K.C. when they made a move at the A's in September; a game against the White Sox that clinched first place; and a late-season game against the Boston Red Sox to "psych" Boston out in case they met in the play-offs." They won all five games.

The Red Sox, always known for their hitting, had

led the majors with a .275 average, and led the A.L. with 756 RBI's while swatting 134 home runs.

They had beaten Baltimore out for first place in the East, led by Fred Lynn and Jim Rice, two of the best rookies ever to come to one team at the same time. Leftfielder Rice had hit .309 with 22 homers and 102 RBI's, while center fielder Lynn had hit .331 with 21 homers and 105 RBI's. Dwight Evans, one of the best defensive players in baseball, completed the outfield.

The infield had been anchored by veteran Carl Yastrzemski at first base. Yaz, who had been one of the best players in baseball in his 15 years with Boston, had injured his shoulder during the season and only batted .269. But despite his 36 years, when the team was in a tight spot, he would usually find a way to win. Because Rice had broken his hand the last week of the season, Yaz had to move back to left field, where he had played for 14 years, and Cecil Cooper, who had hit .311 as the designated hitter, replaced Yaz at first. Second baseman Danny Doyle, who hit .298, provided a solid double-play combination with shortstop Rick Burleson; Rico Petrocelli at third completed the infield. Carlton Fisk provided defense behind the plate and a big bat as shown by his .331 regular-season average. They also had good bench strength in Juan Beniquez and the powerful Bernie Carbo. Their pitching staff was led by starters Luis Tiant (18-14), Rick Wise (19-12), and Bill Lee (17-9), while Roger Moret and Dick Drago were the main men in the bullpen.

If the Sox needed inspiration, Reggie Jackson

may have provided it when he said that he would rather play Boston than Baltimore because the Orioles were used to play-off pressure. "That," said Reggie, "should give us an edge. You can read about it and hear about it, but until you're there you don't know what the pressure is like."

When the game started, though, it was the A's who seemed to feel the pressure as they gave the Sox two runs with the help of three errors. In the seventh, they made another error and added in some sloppy playing and Boston came up with five more runs.

After the game, Reggie said, "It looks like the Jolly Green Giant (Oakland wears green uniforms) was cut down to size. That's the way the Sox are supposed to play." The Sox actually had done their part by committing three errors, which set a play-off record of seven errors in one game. But the three-hit pitching of Luis Tiant had kept the A's bats quiet and Boston beat them 7-1.

But the A's had lost the first game of the play-offs to Baltimore in each of the last two years and had gone on to win, and they were confident of beating Boston. Reggie improved their confidence by hitting a two-run homer in the first and they added another run for a 3-0 lead. Yaz hit a two-run homer and the Sox scored another run to tie the game 3-3 in the fourth. In the sixth, Yaz doubled and scored the winning run off Rollie Fingers, who had had a 3-0 record against Boston during the season. Petrocelli poled a solo homer in the seventh and Lynn added another to complete a 6-3 Boston victory.

After the game, talking about Yaz's hitting and the two great throws that he had made, Reggie said, "Yaz brought them back. All their players hung in there, but Yaz brought them back."

The A's had almost always played their best under pressure as in the 1973 World Series when they had been down three games to two against the Mets and then had come back to beat Tom Seaver in the sixth game and had gone on to take the Series.

But Boston took an early 1-0 lead on an unearned run and added three more in the fifth on three singles, a double by Yaz, and a wild pitch. The A's finally scored one run in the sixth but Boston got another in the top of the eighth. In the bottom of the eighth, the A's made their move. They had one run in and runners on first and second with Reggie at the plate. Reggie lined the ball toward the alley in left center for what looked like a sure triple. But Yaz dove full length at the ball and held Jackson to a single as only one run scored. Dick Drago came in and got Joe Rudi to ground into a double play to end the inning and then shut them down in the ninth.

The Red Sox had dethroned the A's as champions and won the A.L. pennant.

The 72nd World Series was scheduled to begin in Boston's Fenway Park. Fenway, built in 1912, is a very special place in which to play or watch a baseball game. Unlike today's modern stadiums, which are large and all shaped about the same, Fenway Park is small, with a seating capacity of only 32,583, so most fans can be very close to the field. Fenway Park also has a lot of little nooks and oddities that make it a difficult park to play in, especially if you are unfamiliar with it. The most memorable feature in Fenway is the left-field wall, which is known as "The Wall" or, because of the difficulties it presents and the color it is painted, "The Green Monster". The Wall is close to home plate and it is high—37 feet high with a 23-foot screen on top of it.

It is difficult to pitch at Fenway because The Wall is only 315 feet from home plate, which is a short distance for major-league hitters. It presents difficulties on defense, especially to left fielders because, as Gene Mauch, the manager of the Angels, put it, "The ball can bounce off The Wall and go anywhere." And the Green Monster can hurt hitters as well. As Ted Kluszewski, a Cincinnati coach and former major leaguer, puts it, "You see The Wall for the first time and you want to really go for it. But that can mess up your swing."

Boston would have a definite advantage when the games were played at Fenway, but when they moved to Cincinnati, the Red Sox would have to be concerned with the artificial turf at Riverfront Stadium. A ball hit on the turf moves much more quickly than a ball hit on natural grass and that means that it gets to the fielder more quickly. Routine grounders can easily become singles and singles can quickly become doubles or triples.

It promised to be a very exciting series, and no matter which team won, the winning team and city would be v-e-r-y happy. Cincinnati hadn't won a World Series in 35 years and Boston hadn't won in 57 years. Both cities had waited a long time and both teams were thirsty for the taste of victory.

Don Gullett, the starter for the Reds in the first game, told reporters, "I'm not concerned with The Monster. My hard stuff will get the job done."

Gullett and Boston starter Luis Tiant hooked up in a pitching duel and neither team scored for six innings. Both teams mounted threats but clutch pitching and super defense kept the game scoreless. Both Geronimo and Concepcion threw Boston batters out at home plate.

But in the seventh inning, it all began to fall apart for Gullett and the Reds when Tiant singled for his first hit in three years. Next, Gullett fielded a bunt by Evans and while he was throwing to second, he slipped and the ball wound up in center field. Doyle then singled to load the bases and Yaz singled to score Tiant. By the time the inning was over, the Sox had six runs. That was more than enough support for Tiant, who stalled the Big Red Machine by tossing a five-hit shutout against them.

In the second game, Boston scored in the first inning on some odd plays. It began when Foster misplayed a Cecil Cooper line drive into a double. Doyle then beat out an infield single as Cooper went to third. Yaz bounced back to the pitcher, Jack Billingham, who forced Doyle at second, while Cooper tried to score. But Concepcion threw home and Cooper was tagged out in a run-down while Yaz ran to second. The Red Sox finally scored when Fisk singled Yaz home.

The Reds tied it in the fourth, but Boston went ahead 2-1 in the sixth when Yaz and Petrocelli sandwiched singles around an error by Concepcion. Bill Lee took the one-run lead and a four-hitter into the ninth inning, but Bench, looking for an outside pitch, guessed correctly and lined it into right for a double. Dick Drago, who had saved two play-offs games, was brought in to face Perez. Perez grounded out as Bench took third. Foster came to the plate hoping to make up for his fielding mistake in the first inning, but he hit a shallow fly to left and Bench had to hold at third. The Reds were down to their last out as Concepcion prepared to bat. He wanted to make up for his sixth-inning error and he didn't want to make the last out of the game as he had in the first game. "It's not going to happen again," he told himself. It didn't. He hit a high bouncer up the middle for an infield single as Bench scored the tying run. Concepcion then stole second on a very close play and rode home on a double to left center by Ken Griffey. The Reds had come back with two runs in the ninth to take a 3-2 lead. Rawly Eastwick, who had shut the Sox out in the eighth inning, repeated his performance in the ninth and Cincinnati had evened the Series at 1-1.

The Series shifted to Riverfront Stadium for the third game, with Gary Nolan pitching for the Reds and Rick Wise for Boston.

Carlton Fisk opened the scoring for Boston with a home run in the second inning, the first home run by either team in the Series. In the fourth, Perez walked and then surprised everyone by stealing second. He had stolen only one base the entire season. But he could have saved his energy because Bench followed with a home run and the Reds led, 2-1. Concepcion and Geronimo, who together had hit only 11 homers all season long, hit back-to-back homers in the fifth. And after Rose tripled over Lynn's head later in the inning, Jim Burton, a left-hander, was brought in to pitch to Griffey and Morgan, both of whom are left-handed hitters. But Burton walked Griffey (who then stole second) and Morgan hit a sacrifice fly that scored Rose. The Reds led, 5-1, and were feeling pretty good.

Boston scored a run in the sixth off Gary Darcy (Nolan had left the game with a stiff neck) on two walks, a wild pitch, and a sacrifice fly by Lynn. In the seventh, Bernie Carbo, who had started out in the majors with Cincinnati, hit a pinch homer to cut the Reds' lead to 5-3. In the ninth, Dwight Evans hit a two-run homer and Boston had come back to tie the game! Now the Reds were feeling pretty lame.

Geronimo began the tenth inning with a walk and George Armbrister was sent up to bunt him to second. What happened next caused a commotion that still excites baseball fans in Boston. Armbrister bunted, Carlton Fisk pounced on it, and threw toward second. Because Armbrister didn't move, he and Fisk collided and the throw went into center field. Fisk argued—and many experts agreed—that Armbrister should have been called out for interference. The umpires disagreed and the Reds wound up with runners at second and third. Southpaw Roger Moret was brought in to walk Rose intentionally (which would load the bases to set up a force play at home) and to pitch to the next two batters, who were left-handed. Anderson crossed up the strategy by sending up Rettenmund, a righty, to hit for Griffey, but Moret fanned him anyway for the first out. Joe Morgan came up next and smacked a tremendous drive to left center and Geronimo trotted home with the winning run. So much for strategy. The Reds were feeling *very* good!

Neither team had hit a homer in cozy Fenway Park, but in spacious Riverfront Stadium, they tied a Series record by hammering out six of them. Baseball can be a funny game.

The Reds began romping in the very first inning of game four off Luis Tiant, who had shut them out in the first game. Rose started it with a single and came home to score on a double by Griffey. A strong relay by Burleson caught Griffey at third when he tried to stretch the hit into a triple. Morgan, though, followed with a walk and Bench doubled him home for a 2-0 lead.

Reds pitcher Fred Norman cruised along for three

innings but in the fourth, the roof caved in. First Fisk singled to left and Lynn singled to right. After an out, Evans tripled home both runners to tie the game. Burleson knocked in Evans with what should have been a single, but alert and aggressive base running stretched it into a double. Borbon came in and Tiant greeted him with a single—his second hit in three years—and Burleson took third. Perez then bobbled Beniquez's grounder and Burleson scored while Tiant moved to second. Yaz delivered a two-out single and Tiant scored the fifth run of the inning.

Before Boston had a chance to feel too good about their 5-2 lead, the Reds, with the help of poor Sox fielding, bounced back with two runs in the bottom of the inning. Foster singled with two out and moved to second on an error. Concepcion hit a blooper to left center that fell between three Boston players for a double while Foster scored. Geronimo then hit a ball that bounced in front of Beniquez in left and then over his head for a triple as Concepcion scored.

The score was still 5-4 in favor of Boston as the Reds came to bat in the bottom of the ninth. Geronimo led with a single and was bunted to second. Rose walked and Griffey hit a drive deep to center where Lynn made a spectacular, over-the-shoulder catch while running at full speed. There were two outs now and Joe Morgan was up with a chance to win the game. But little Joe wouldn't be the hero today. Tiant got him to pop up to Yaz for his second victory. The Series was tied, 2-2.

Boston scored in the opening inning of game five on a triple by Doyle and a sacrifice fly by Yaz. The Reds threatened in their turn at bat but Beniquez threw Rose out at home. They tied it in the fourth, though, when Perez broke out of an 0-15 slump with a home run; and they made it 2-1 in the fifth when Gullett singled with two out and Rose doubled him home. In the sixth inning, Morgan walked and scooted to third on a hit-and-run single by Bench. Three pitches later, Perez poled his second homer of the game and the Reds led, 5-1.

The Reds scored another run in the eighth and Gullett, who was pitching a two-hitter, took a 6-1 lead into the ninth. He retired the first two batters, but then Yaz and Fisk singled and Lynn doubled Yaz home. Rawly Eastwick, who had won games two and three in relief, came in to save the game for Gullett by getting Petrocelli with a strike-out on three straight pitches. The Reds needed one more win.

The teams returned to Boston for game six, which turned out to be one of the most exciting games in World Series history. For many people, especially Bostonians, it became known simply as THE GAME.

Boston had to win to force a seventh game and they struck early. In the first inning, Yaz and Fisk each rapped two-out singles. Fred Lynn, who had not hit much during the Series, came up and hit the ball long and high and over the Boston bullpen in right center for a three-run homer. The fans in Fenway loved it.

The Reds, though, evened matters in the fifth

when a walk, a Pete Rose single, and a long triple off the center-field wall by Griffey produced two runs, and a Johnny Bench single off The Wall in left scored Griffey.

Griffey and Morgan both singled to left to start the seventh but Tiant got Bench and Perez to fly out. George Foster, though, came through with a 400-foot blast for a double and both runners scored. Geronimo hit a homer in the eighth to make it 6-3 and the Reds were ready to celebrate. As Tiant was taken out of the game, he felt gloomy despite the standing ovation that he received from the Boston fans.

The Sox were down to their last six outs as Lynn opened the eighth with a single. Petrocelli walked but then Rawly Eastwick came in and retired the next two batters. Bernie Carbo came up now to pinch-hit against the team that had traded him. In game two, Eastwick had fanned him. This time, as the crowd sat tense, the count went to three-and-two. Eastwick delivered, Carbo swung, and the ball rocketed into the center-field bleachers for a three-run homer. The Fenway fans went wild; the game was tied, 6-6.

In the ninth inning, the Sox loaded the bases with nobody out and Lynn came up to bat. He only managed to lift a short fly to left and when Doyle tried to tag up, Foster threw him out. Petrocelli made the third out and Boston had wasted a golden opportunity. So now they were going to extra innings.

In the 11th, Rose led off by being hit with a pitch. Griffey tried to bunt him into scoring position but Fisk pounced on the ball and forced Rose at second. Morgan came up and smacked a long fly to right field. Evans raced back as the ball headed for the stands, and at the last second, he leaped up and made a spectacular, one-handed catch to rob Morgan of a home run. Then he threw the ball into the infield and Griffey, who was already at third, was doubled up. In the wink of an eye, a game that looked to be lost was saved, for now anyway.

Bench led off the 12th by hitting a high pop foul on which Fisk made a remarkable catch while leaning into the stands. Perez and Foster singled out but Rick Wise got Concepcion on a fly and fanned Geronimo.

Carlton Fisk led off the bottom of the 12th by hitting the first pitch deep down the left-field line. If it stayed fair, it was gone. As Fisk saw the ball sail toward the seats, it began to hook. As he watched the ball come down, he twisted his body as though he could will it to stay fair. And then it landed high up against the foul pole; it was a home run. Boston had won 7-6; the Series was all even. Carlton jumped in the air and did a little jig on his way to first. As he circled the bases, Boston fans raced on to the field and Carlton had to push his way to home plate.

Even though his team lost, Sparky Anderson appreciated the quality of the game. "It was probably as good a game as I've seen. And that catch by Evans was as good a catch as you'll see." Joe Morgan saw things from a different perspective. "I was out there looking to win. We had the championship within our grasp and let it slip away. But we'll be back tomorrow night."

Pete Rose, though, probably summed up the game best for most of the players and fans at Fenway and the millions who watched it on TV when he said, "I don't think that anybody can ask for a better game than this. It had more ups and downs than any game in my life."

Boston took an early lead in the final game with three runs in the third inning. Carbo, starting in left field, drew a one-out walk and moved to third on Doyle's single. Yaz singled Carbo home and took second as Griffey tried but failed to throw Doyle out at third. Gullett walked Fisk so that the southpaw could pitch to lefty Fred Lynn and the strategy worked perfectly as Gullett struck out Lynn for the second out. But then he lost his control and gave up bases-loaded walks to Petrocelli and Evans. After the inning, Petrocelli walked out to third base, thinking, *We have it. This is our year.*

The Reds threatened in most innings but didn't score against Bill Lee until the sixth. Pete Rose started it with a single and after Morgan flied out, Bench grounded to Burleson for what should have been an inning-ending double play. But they only got the force on Rose because he slid into Doyle at second, which caused Doyle to throw wildly to first. Then Perez came up and hit a two-run homer over The Wall. They tied the game in the seventh on an RBI single and had a chance to blow Boston away, but Bench fouled out to Fisk with two outs and the bases loaded.

Rookie southpaw Jim Burton came in to pitch the eighth and walked Griffey. Geronimo sacrificed him to second and a ground-out moved him to third with two out. On a 3-2 pitch, Rose walked. Morgan came up and the count went to 1-2. Burton threw a slider low and away from the left-handed Morgan, who swung and hit the ball off the end of his bat. It was a softly hit ball that fell just out of the reach of the hard-charging Fred Lynn. Griffey scored from third as the Reds took a 4-3 lead. Both Burton and Morgan agreed that it had been a good pitch. "Two years ago, I would have struck out on it," said Joe, after the game.

In the ninth, Will McEnany quickly retired two pinch-hitters and then up to the plate came Yaz. In his 15 years with Boston, Yaz had won countless ballgames that seemed lost. He stepped into the batter's box and cocked his bat. McEnany made his pitch and Yaz swung and lifted a fly ball to center that settled in Geronimo's glove.

And just like that, the game and the World Series were over. Two splendid teams had battled each other to the final out and had provided baseball fans everywhere with a Series to warm their memories.

Pete Rose was ecstatic. "I've never won anything before. I've never won an American Legion championship. I never won a high school championship." Pete had his championship and, after a 35-year wait, so did the city of Cincinnati. It had been a long time coming!

CHAPTER 3

It's Never Over
Until It's Over

In the year 1985, some of the greatest baseball players in history reached career milestones. Pete Rose stroked hit Number 4,192, breaking the record for most hits in a career, which had been set by Ty Cobb and had gone unchallenged since 1928! Nolan Ryan became the only pitcher to record 4,000 strike-outs. Rod Carew became only the 16th player in history to get 3,000 hits; Tom Seaver became only the 17th pitcher to record 300 victories; and on the last day of the season, 46-year-old Phil Niekro became the 18th when he shut out the Toronto Blue Jays. (He also became the oldest player ever to pitch a shutout in the major leagues.)

It was also a year of achievement for younger players such as: Vince Coleman, who established a new base-stealing record for rookies by swiping 110; and Dwight Gooden, the phenomenal pitcher for the Mets, who established all sorts of records and became the youngest pitcher ever to win 20 games in a season. (He wound up 24-4).

Nineteen eighty-five was also a year of exciting divisional races (three of the four weren't decided until the next-to-last day of the season) that produced four surprise winners. Most experts thought that California or Chicago would take the American League West, while Detroit, who had pulverized the A.L. East in 1984 and gone on to win the World Series, was considered likely to repeat. In the National League, San Diego was picked to repeat in the West, while in the East, it looked as if the Cubs would battle it out with the Mets. The experts were in for a surprise.

The Kansas City Royals won the A.L. West over California by beating the Angels three out of four games in the last week of the season. Their opponents in the league championship series were the Toronto Blue Jays, who captured their first divisional title. They held off a late charge by the Yankees by beating them on the next-to-last day of the season to win the A.L. East. In the National League, the Cubs were never a factor and the St. Louis Cardinals won by holding off the Mets in another close race. The L.A.

Dodgers, winners in the National League West, were the only team to coast in, as they finished a comfortable five and one-half games in front of Cincinnati.

Kansas City was viewed as the weakest of the four play-off teams. Their offense was almost totally dependent upon George Brett, their all-star third baseman. During the season, Brett had batted .335 (second best to Wade Boggs's .368 in the A.L.), hit 30 homers, and driven in 112 runs. First baseman Steve Balboni had provided power with 36 homers, but hit only .243. Hal McRae, the DH (designated hitter), centerfielder Willie Wilson, and second baseman Frank White, who, along with Brett, formed the nucleus of the offense, had all had disappointing seasons. The team batting average was next to last in the A.L. They did, however, have a fine group of starting pitchers, led by Bret Saberhagen (20-6) and Charlie Leibrandt (17-9), as well as veteran reliever Dan Quisenberry, who led the A.L. with 37 saves.

The only problem for K.C. was that Toronto also had fine pitching as well as the second-highest team batting average in the majors. Their outfield was especially strong as George Bell (left), Lloyd Moseby (center), and Jesse Barfield (right) had combined for 73 homers and 249 RBI's.

In Game 1, Leibrandt, who had been 2-0 against the Jays during the season, started against Toronto ace Dave Stieb, who had been 0-3 against K.C. Naturally, Toronto lowered the boom on Leibrandt by scoring five runs within the first three innings, while Stieb limited the Royals to three hits in eight innings. Toronto coasted to a 6-1 win as the eighth and ninth hitters, catcher Ernie Witt and short-stop Tony Fernandez, each knocked in a pair of runs.

In game two, Willie Wilson gave K.C. an early lead with a two-run homer and catcher Jim Sundberg doubled home another run for a 3-0 lead. Toronto came back to tie the game with the help of errors by Brett and pitcher Bud Black and a two-run single by Barfield. The Jays took the lead in the eighth when Moseby came in to score after he singled, stole second, and went to third on a bad throw by Sundberg. In the top of the ninth, though, pinch hitter Pat Sheridan put one over the fence to tie the game. In the top of the tenth, Willie Wilson singled, stole second, and scored the go-ahead run on a single by Frank White. K.C. needed only three outs to even the play-offs and they had Quisenberry, who had three saves against the Jays in the regular season, in there to do the job. But Fernandez singled and came around to score on a Moseby single to tie the game. Moseby advanced on an error by Balboni when Quisenberry tried a pick-off play, and pinch hitter Al Oliver singled him home with the winning run. The extra-inning, come-from-behind win gave Toronto a 2-0 lead and put K.C. on thin ice.

But George Brett put on an amazing performance in game three to put K.C. on safer footing. He began by homering in the first and then doubled and scored in the fourth to give K.C. a 2-0 lead. Toronto stormed back, though, with five in the fifth. Barfield got them going with a two-run homer. Damaso Garcia doubled and Moseby followed with a hard smash that hit the heel of Saberhagen's left foot and then bounced into the outfield. Garcia raced home while Saberhagen lay on the ground in obvious pain. The next batter was Rance Mulliniks, who hit another two-run homer as Toronto took a 5-2 lead and Saberhagen left the game. After Sundberg hit a homer to cut the lead to 5-3, Brett hit a two-run homer to tie the game in the sixth. In the eighth, Brett did it again as he doubled and scored the winning run on a bloop hit by Balboni. After the game, K.C. manager Dick Howser said of Brett, "That's a Hall of Fame performance." That performance provided Howser with his first play-off victory after 11 straight losses.

Game four was a tense pitching duel between Stieb and Leibrandt. Going into the ninth, K.C. had a one-run lead and Leibrandt had a four-hitter. But Garcia walked and Moseby doubled him home to tie the game. Quisenberry came in to pitch and Bell greeted him with a single. Al Oliver followed with a two-run double and Toronto had pulled off a 3-1 victory—they now needed only one more win.

K.C. was back on thin ice but just as it was beginning to crack, Danny Jackson froze Toronto's bats and K.C. won the fifth game, 2-0.

In the sixth game, Hal McRae knocked in a run in the first and another in the third inning, but Toronto matched them. Brett put K.C. in front for good in the fifth, however, with a homer, and the Royals scored two more in the sixth on their way to a 5-3 victory.

The pennant chase had come down to one game now and each team had its ace pitcher ready: Saberhagen for K.C. and Stieb for Toronto. But Saberhagen had to depart after three innings due to an injury and Stieb left after five and two-thirds innings because K.C. had rocked him for six runs. Jim Sundberg did the most damage with a homer, triple, and four RBI's as K.C. went on to score a 6-2 victory. The Royals had been expected to lose and had been down three games to one, but they had just kept playing as hard as they could and it was Toronto who wound up in the deep freeze while K.C. skated away with the A.L. pennant.

The Cardinals, who led the majors with 101 victories, were ready for the play-offs. Their offense combined good hitting (they tied for the league lead) with blazing speed (a league-leading 314 stolen bases). Vince Coleman, the lead-off hitter, had 110 stolen bases; he was followed by Willie McGee, who led the league in hitting (.353), drove in 82 runs, and swiped 56 bases. Tommy Herr, batting third, hit .302 and knocked in 110 runs, and Jim Clark, the cleanup hitter, smacked 22 homers and drove in 87, even though he missed a month with an injury. Their defense, which committed the fewest errors in the N.L., was anchored at shortstop by the acrobatic Ozzie Smith. He's so spectacular that he's known as the "Wizard of

Oz" for the magical way that he plays the position. John Tudor (21-8), Joaquin Andujar (21-12), and Danny Cox (18-9) were the leading starters. And Manager Whitey Herzog had five strong relief pitchers who were referred to as "The Committee," as well as strong reserves on the bench.

The Dodgers didn't appear to be quite as strong but they had two hitters, Pedro Guerrero (.320 average with 33 homers and 87 RBI's) and Mike Marshall (.293, 28, 95), who could carry a team in a short series. Their pitching staff had the best earned-run average in the majors. It had three fine starters in Orel Hershiser (19-3), Fernando Valenzuela (17-10), and Bob Welch (14-4). The main man in the bullpen was flame-throwing Tom Niedenfuer.

In game one, the Dodgers jumped to a 4-0 lead off John Tudor, who had won 11 straight games. Valenzuela shut down the Cardinals' running game by keeping Coleman and McGee off the bases. When Valenzuela weakened in the seventh and allowed a run, Niedenfuer came in and got a double play. He shut the Cards down the rest of the way and the Dodgers won, 4-1.

In game two, Coleman and McGee each got on base in the first inning, but they were both thrown out trying to steal. As Herzog said after the game, "You rely on speed, you live dangerously; but that's what got us into the play-offs." McGee did use his speed to get the first run of the game in the third when he scored all the way from second on a wild pitch. But the Dodgers answered with three in the bottom of the inning off Andujar and went on to an 8-2 romp. They now led 2-0, but Herzog wasn't overly concerned. "We're capable of winning four in a row. We just didn't play very good ball in L.A."

In game three, Coleman used his speed to help the Cards score twice and Herr hit a home run as the Cards built an early 4-0 lead. The Cards held on to win 4-2 behind the solid pitching of Danny Cox and The Committee and the sensational fielding of third baseman Terry Pendleton. Pendleton snuffed out a Dodger rally in the ninth when, with no outs and a runner on second, he made a back-handed, sprawling stab of what looked like a sure double and turned it into an out. As Dodger manager Tommy LaSorda said later, "That one changed the game."

Before the start of game four, Vince Coleman suffered an injury to his leg in a freak accident and was out of action. But his replacement, Tito Landrum, went four-for-five as the Cards rocked the Dodgers, 12-2. They broke the game open in the second by scoring nine runs (the most runs ever scored in one inning in a play-off game), and John Tudor kept the Dodgers hitters in check. The play-offs were now tied, 2-2.

The Cards took the lead in game five when Tommy Herr doubled home two runs in the first inning. Valenzuela gave up eight walks, a play-off record, but he lasted eight innings without allowing another run. The Dodgers tied the game in the fourth

on a two-run homer over the left-field fence by Bill
Madlock. Niedenfuer was brought in to pitch to the
Cards in the bottom of the ninth and retired the first
batter. The next batter was Ozzie Smith. Oz looked
overmatched against the large, hard-throwing reliever,
but he smacked a fastball into the right-field stands
and the Cards won, 3-2. In his eight years in the majors, the switch-hitting Oz had hit only 13 homers and
had never before hit one while batting from the left
side. As he said happily after the game, "Sometimes
the most unlikely hero emerges."

The Dodgers now trailed 3-2 and needed a win
to keep their pennant hopes alive. They struck early
and enjoyed a 4-1 lead into the seventh, but a two-run
single by McGee cut the lead to 4-3. Niedenfuer was
brought in to replace Hershiser and protect the lead.
The first batter, though, was Oz, and he lined a triple
down the right-field line that sent McGee in with the
tying run. Niedenfuer was beginning to think that
Babe Ruth must have sneaked into Oz's uniform.

Mike Marshall got the go-ahead run for L.A. in
the eighth inning with a long home run. The Cards
rallied in the ninth, though, when McGee singled and
Oz walked. Jim Clark came up, remembering that
earlier in the play-off, "Niedenfuer had blown me
away." Niedenfuer decided to try and make Clark
chase a bad pitch but first, "I tried to get away with
a fastball to get ahead in the count." The pitch came
toward the plate. "I saw the ball real well. I saw the
rotation on the seam," said Clark. Clark swung and

sent the ball sailing over the fence for a three-run home run. The Cards won the game, 7-5. They had captured the National League pennant.

St. Louis had beaten back the challenge of the Mets and then gone on to defeat the Dodgers soundly. Kansas City had had to struggle to win in the weakest division and then just managed to squeak by the Blue Jays. And now they would lose the regular services of their cleanup hitter, Hal McRae, because the designated hitter wouldn't be eligible in the World Series in 1985. It looked as if K.C. had gone about as far as they could go. Danny Jackson, named to start the opening game of the World Series, summed up the situation. "We know we're the underdogs. They've got speed, they can hit, they score runs, they've got good pitching. But we'll go with our best stuff and take it from there."

Their best stuff wasn't good enough for game one. After they opened the scoring with a run off John Tudor, he shut them out the rest of the way, and RBI's by McGee, Cedeno, and Jack Clark gave St. Louis the opening game, 3-1.

In the second game, Charlie Leibrandt pitched beautifully for K.C. and had a 1-0 lead and a two-hitter going into the ninth inning. McGee, though, opened the ninth by doubling past third. But Leibrandt got Smith to ground to third and Herr to pop to right. One more out to go. Jack Clark was the next batter, and he singled in McGee to tie the game. Tito Landrum, playing for the still injured Vince Coleman, doubled on a 2-2 pitch and Clark went to third. After an intentional walk, Terry Pendleton doubled home three more runs. Quisenberry was brought in and finally got the third out, but Jeff Lahti retired K.C. in the bottom of the ninth and the Cards won, 4-2. Just like that, Leibrandt had lost his shutout and then the game.

After the game, there were a lot of questions and opinions as to whether Dan Quisenberry should have been brought in sooner. K.C.'s manager, Dick Howser, naturally didn't think so. "Charlie was in complete control. His stuff was great. I liked the way he was pitching." Whitey Herzog, the manager of the Cardinals, sympathized. "Clark didn't murder that pitch, Tito hit his double off the end of the bat, and Pendleton was jammed and just got his bat on it. We didn't hit the ball well. Leibrandt deserved to win. I guess sometimes things just happen funny."

But the Kansas City players weren't doing any laughing, especially Charlie Leibrandt, and now they were down 2-0. No team had ever lost the first two games at home and then gone on to win a World Series.

The Cards, though, were dealt a bad hand before game three even began when they learned that Vince Coleman's injury would keep him out of the rest of the Series. K.C. added to their bad deal when Lonnie Smith doubled home two runs in the fourth and Frank White followed a George Brett single with a home run in the fifth. The Cards managed to score a run in the sixth, but that was the only one that Saberhagen allowed, as K.C. coasted to their first win, 6-1.

After the game, Saberhagen told reporters, "I was really nervous in the first inning. It was a big game for us."

John Tudor made everyone on the Royals really nervous after the fourth game because he threw a five-hit shutout at them while Tito Landrum and Willie McGee homered and the Cards won, 3-0. Tudor was overpowering. As George Brett, who struck out twice, said, "It was embarrassing."

Down three games to one, K.C. really had their backs against the wall. One more loss and they could start their winter vacations. But Dan Quisenbery was able to offer a humorous point of view. "I wish that we could do it some other way, but we've done it this way all year, so what's new? If we're going to win it, this would be the way to do it."

Howser gave the ball to Danny Jackson to keep the Series alive for K.C. as he had done in game five against Toronto, and Jackson came through again. He allowed only a first-inning run while K.C. rocked the Cards for six runs, including Willie Wilson's two-run triple. It was a strange game, though, because St. Louis pitchers, led by Todd Worrell's record-tying 6 in a row, struck out 15 K.C. batters. The Cards had the strike-outs but K.C. had the win and had cut their deficit to 3-2.

In game six, Whitey Herzog started Danny Cox. He had beaten the Mets in the last week of the season when a Mets victory would have tied them with the Cards. And he beat the Dodgers in game three of the N.L. championship series after the Dodgers had taken the first two. Howser answered with Charlie Leibrandt and for seven innings, neither team could score. In the bottom of the eighth, though, Leibrandt slipped a little bit and the Cards pushed across a run with two out before Quisenberry came in to get the third out.

The Royals were now down to their last three outs. To win, they would have to overcome an amazing record—through 84 games of the regular season and 7 post-season games, St. Louis hadn't lost a single game in which they had taken a lead into the ninth inning. Pinch-hitter Jorge Orta started the inning by hitting a chopper wide of first, and with a burst of speed, just beat it out. Herzog jumped up to argue the ump's call, but, of course, he lost the argument. Then Balboni was given a second chance when Clark couldn't get to his foul pop-up, and he came through with a single. Sundberg tried to sacrifice the runners but Worrell came off the mound quickly and forced Orta at third. McRae pinch-hit and was intentionally walked to load the bases. Dane Iorg, an ex-Cardinal, was sent up to pinch-hit for Quisenberry.

"That's a situation you dream about as a kid," Iorg would say after the game. "All my life, I've dreamed about hitting with the bases loaded in the ninth inning with a chance to win the game." Iorg took the first pitch for a ball. Worrell checked the runners and then burned a fastball inside that jammed Iorg, but he fought the pitch off and hit a soft line drive into right field. Concepcion, running for Balboni, scored from third to tie the game. Iorg, already at first, turned to look at Sundberg racing toward home, and Porter, blocking the plate, waiting for Van Slyke's throw. Iorg said, "I saw Sunny sliding and scoring and that's when I felt the thrill."

Kansas City had tied the Series and Bret Saberhagen sat in the dugout thinking, "Now it's my turn. Then I almost beat Sundberg to the plate I was so happy."

In the other clubhouse, Todd Worrell, the losing pitcher, wasn't happy, but he wasn't breaking furniture or complaining about the umpiring, or Clark's not catching Balboni's foul pop. He realized that he had pitched well and gained valuable experience in a pressure situation. And, he realized, "You can't always be a winner."

Game seven was expected to be a pitching duel with Saberhagen going against John Tudor. But Tudor, who had been the Cards' best and most reliable pitcher all season, didn't have it that day. He walked Balboni in the second and Darryl Motley followed with a two-run homer. Tudor, a control pitcher, walked the bases loaded in the third and George Brett accidently singled for a run while trying to avoid being hit by a pitch. Bill Campbell came in to relieve but Balboni singled for two more runs, and then in the sixth, Kansas City erupted for six more. Saberhagen never let the Cardinals back into the game. He allowed no walks and only five harmless singles as the Royals romped, 11-0.

While the team celebrated their victory, people searched for explanations. Some pointed to the pitching staff, which had shut down the Cardinals' awesome running game, while limiting them to only 13 runs in the seven games. Many of the players, including Frank White, pointed to Dick Howser and the coaching staff. "He didn't criticize us when we weren't hitting." And Charlie Leibrant noted, "This coaching staff is all positive, all upbeat. It's the kind of team I like to play for."

The 1985 Royals were a special kind of team. Maybe, as Whitey Herzog suggested, they weren't a great team. Maybe he was right when he said that they wouldn't have been good enough even to win one of the other three divisions. But people had been telling them that they weren't good enough since spring training, told them that in the middle of the season when they were seven and one-half games behind California, and again when they trailed in the last week of the season. But they came back to win the division *and* the pennant *and* the World Series after being down 3-1 each time. They never gave up on themselves; they never quit. And because of that, Danny Jackson could scream happily, "We shocked the world!"

CHAPTER 4

Most Amazing

A funny thing almost happened to the Boston Red Sox and the New York Mets on their way to the 1986 World Series—they almost watched the California Angels play the Houston Astros!

Before the Red Sox and the Mets could meet in the World Series, the Red Sox had to beat the California Angels to win the American League pennant, and the Mets had to defeat the Houston Astros to capture the National League flag.

No problem, right? W R O N G !

In the two wildest championship series since the play-off system was first begun in 1969, California and Houston stretched Boston and New York to their limits before going down to defeat. Boston, in fact, came within one single strike of losing the play-offs, while the Mets had to eke out some very exciting wins—including the longest game in play-off history—before they were able to defeat the Astros.

Both of the series will be long remembered by everyone who cares about baseball.

The Red Sox traditionally have been a strong hitting team and 1986 was no exception. Third baseman Wade Boggs, who had won three of the last four A.L. batting titles, led both leagues with a regular-season average of .357. Following Boggs in the line-up were sluggers such as Jim Rice, who hit .304 while stroking 20 homers and knocking in 115 runs; first baseman Bill Buckner, who had 18 home runs and 102 RBI's; right fielder Dwight Evans, who poled 26 home runs and had 97 runs batted in; and Don Baylor, the designated hitter, who had 31 home runs and 94 RBI's.

In 1986, the Red Sox also had something they usually lacked—a strong pitching staff, which was led by Roger Clemens. Clemens had achieved a sparkling 24-4 record during the regular season, which included a record-setting performance in which he struck out 20 batters in a single game! He was easily the best pitcher in the A.L. And he had support from other starters such as Bruce Hurst and the exciting Dennis "Oil Can" Boyd. When the starters needed help, Calvin Schiraldi, the young, hard-throwing relief pitcher would march in from the bullpen.

California was a team made up mostly of older players such as Reggie Jackson, Bobby Grich, Doug DeCinces, and Don Sutton—whose best years in baseball were behind them. No one really expected them to put up much of a fight against the younger and stronger Red Sox.

But somebody forgot to tell that to the Angels and they came within a single pitch of taking the pennant, four games to one.

In game one, the Angels shocked the Red Sox by pounding out an 8-1 victory; and they did it in Boston and against Roger Clemens. Brian Downing, who had four RBI's in the game, and the other Angels showed no respect for Roger's regular-season record.

In game two, the Sox bounced back, 9-2, behind the solid pitching of Bruce Hurst. The game was so full of errors and mental mistakes that Don Sutton remarked, "The last time I saw a game like this, our [little league] coach wouldn't take us to Tastee-Freeze for a milkshake afterwards."

The play-off series moved to sunny California but the Angels were poor hosts as they beat Boston 5-3 and took a 2-1 lead in the play-offs. Shortstop Dick Shofield and center fielder Gary Pettis, who are not usually long-ball hitters, each stroked a home run off losing pitcher Oil Can Boyd.

Boston's manager, John McNamara, sent Roger Clemens out to the mound to try and even the Series. Roger shut the Angels out for eight innings and took a 3-0 lead into the ninth inning. He needed only three more outs, but he never got them.

Doug DeCinces led off with a home run, and after Clemens retired a batter, Dick Schofield and Bob Boone singled. Clemens was taken out of the game and Calvin Schiraldi was brought in to put out the fire. But Jim Rice lost a fly ball in the lights that allowed one run to score and put runners on second and third. The next batter was walked intentionally and then Schiraldi struck out Bobby Grich for the second out. Calvin then got two quick strikes on Brian Downing. As Brian said after the game, "He had me in real trouble. I was in a hole and he knew it." But then Calvin tried to put too much on a curve ball and the pitch hit Downing, which allowed the tying run to cross the plate.

In the 11th inning, Bobby Grich singled in the winning run off Calvin and the Angels—"the Over-the-Hill Gang"—led the play-off series, 3-1. One more victory and the Angels would win the A.L. pennant from the stunned Red Sox.

In the very next game, California led 5-2 in the top of the ninth inning and were only three outs away from winning the first pennant in their 26-year history. And they had Mike Witt, their best pitcher on the mound.

With one out, though, Don Baylor cracked a two-run homer to cut the lead to 5-4. Two pitches later, Dave Henderson, with a 2-2 count, crashed another two-run homer and Boston now led, 6-5.

California came back to tie the game in the bottom of the ninth on super base running by Gary Pettis. But losing that three-run lead in the top of the 9th seemed to have taken the fire out of the Angels, and Boston won it in the 11th when Dave Henderson hit a sacrifice fly to drive in Don Baylor with the winning run. Calvin Schiraldi, who had let the Angels tie and then win the day before, retired the Angels in order in the bottom of the inning.

After the game, Don Baylor said, "I'm still emotionally high. I've never been involved in a game like this before. We were one pitch away from a long winter."

A smiling John McNamara remarked, "That baseball game was the best baseball game, the most competitive game, I've ever seen."

The teams traveled back to Boston to finish the series but California was never really able to recover from that fifth-game loss. Boston pounded out 16 hits to take the sixth game, 10-4, and clinched the series when Roger Clemens finally earned a play-off victory in an 8-1 yawn of a game.

After 14 years of managing, John McNamara had his first pennant. Bring on the National League!

The 1986 Mets were an awesome team. They had charged into first place on April 23 and stayed there for the rest of the season. On their way to the Eastern Division title, they had won 108 games and finished $21^1/_2$ games in front of the second-place team, the Philadelphia Phillies. Amazing!

The Astros were a solid team at every position with good hitting, speed, and defense, and a fine pitching staff. They had had to work a lot harder than the Mets did to clinch their divisional title but by the end of the season they were on a roll. Still, most baseball watchers didn't give them much of a chance against the high-flying Mets.

The Mets, however, were brought down to earth quickly as the Astros beat them 1-0 in the play-off opener. Astro first baseman Glenn Davis, who had led the team in homers with 31 during the regular season, supplied the power with a second-inning homer off Met ace Dwight Gooden. And Mike Scott, the top pitcher in the National League in 1986, supplied the pitching, as he not only shut out the Mets but also struck out 14 to tie a play-off record.

Mike Scott, who had led the N.L. in strike-outs (306) and ERA (2.22), and who had pitched a no-hitter on the night that the Astros clinched the divisional title, completely mastered the Mets with his split-fingered fastball. Lenny Dykstra, the Mets' center fielder, expressed the view of most of the players when he said, "I've never seen anything like it in my life. It's like a whiffle ball moving in the wind."

The Mets evened the series with a 5-1 victory as Bob Ojeda, an 18-game winner during the regular season, outpitched 39-year-old Nolan Ryan, the all-time major-league leader in strike-outs with 4,277. Keith Hernandez, the Mets' great fielding and clutch-hitting first baseman, led the attack with two hits and two runs batted in. It is interesting to note that both Mike Scott and Nolan Ryan had begun their big-league careers with the Mets. (Ryan was traded to the Angels and wound up with the Astros later on, while Scott was dealt directly to the Astros for outfielder Danny Heep.)

Game three was a thriller. The Astros took an early four-run lead off Met starter Ron Darling, with two runs in the first and two more in the second, thanks to a Bill Doran homer. The Mets fought back, though, and in the sixth inning, tied the game with the help of a three-run home run by outfielder Darryl Strawberry. Strawberry hit the homer off Astro starter Bob Knepper after going hitless (0-10) against him in the regular season. Houston regained the lead in the seventh when they scored a run off Met reliever Rick Aguilera. The Astros took that slim lead into the ninth inning and handed the ball to Dave Smith, their ace reliever. Wally Backman, the Mets' scrappy second baseman, began the inning by dragging a bunt for a single. That brought up Lenny Dykstra. (Dykstra is small and thin but his nickname is "Nails", as in the expression "as tough as nails." He doesn't quit.) Dykstra found a pitch to his liking and promptly drilled a game-winning two-run homer to give the Mets a scintillating 6-5 win. The fans at Shea stood and cheered as Dykstra scored the run that gave the Mets a two-to-one lead in games.

In game four, the Mets finally managed to score a run off Mike Scott, but it wasn't enough and they lost, 3-1. Catcher Alan Ashby and shortstop Dickie Thon each homered off Met starter and loser Sid Fernandez. The play-off was tied, 2-2.

Game five was a real nail-biter as 21-year-old Dwight Gooden matched fastballs and curveballs with 39-year-old Nolan Ryan in a tense pitching duel. Ryan was magnificent during his nine innings as he struck

1—Babe Ruth hitting a home run in the 1932 World Series right after he had pointed his bat to the center field stands.

2—Enos Slaughter sliding home safely with the winning run in the seventh game of the 1946 Series. He galloped all the way from first on a single as the Cardinals beat the Red Sox.

3—Don Larsen throwing the final strike in the only
perfect game ever pitched in a World Series. It was
the fifth game of the 1956 Series and Dale Mitchell
was the last batter.

4—*Johnny Podres winding up to retire Elston Howard, the last batter of the 1955 World Series.*

5—Jerry Koosman on the mound during the fifth and final game for the Mets in 1969. They beat Baltimore four games to one.

6—Carlton Fisk blasts a home run.

7—Tony Perez starting Cincinnati on the way to victory in the seventh game with a 2-run homer.

8—*Reggie Jackson hitting the second of his three homers in the final game of the 1977 World Series. The Yanks beat the L.A. Dodgers four games to two.*

9—Royals ace, Bret Saberhagen, beats the Cards in 1985.

10— Keith Hernandez demonstrates perfect form as he delivers a key hit in game six against Boston.

11— *Ray Knight hitting a seventh inning homer in the seventh game to give the Mets the lead.*

COURTESY OF THE MINNESOTA TWINS BASEBALL CLUB.

12—*It's Sweet Music for the Twins as Frank Viola tames the Cards.*

13—Kirk Gibson watches his game-winning
home run in Game One of the 1988 Series.
Courtesy Los Angeles Dodgers.

14—Orel Hershiser is King of the Hill. *Courtesy Los Angeles Dodgers.*

15—Dave Stewart shows his winning form in game 3 victory over the Giants in 1989 World Series.

16—Jose Canseco gets double-barreled Bash Brothers treatment from Rickey Henderson (24) and Carney Lansford after stroking 3-run homer against the Giants.

out 12 batters while giving up only two hits, including a fifth-inning homer by Darryl Strawberry. Gooden was not quite as spectacular, but he pitched courageously for ten innings—the longest that he had ever pitched—and left the game with the score tied, 1-1.

The Mets finally broke through for the winning run in the 12th inning when their catcher, Gary Carter, who was in a terrible batting slump (1-21), lined a single to score Wally Backman. Jesse Orosco, with two perfect innings of relief work, picked up his second victory.

The Mets were now ahead in the play-offs, 3-2, and needed to win only one of the last two games. But they knew that if they didn't win game six, they would have to face Mike Scott in the final game. The Mets didn't want to face Mike Scott again.

Game six would prove to be the most exciting play-off game ever, and like the fifth game of the Red Sox-Angels series, it will be remembered and talked about for as long as people enjoy baseball.

The Mets fell behind early, as the usually dependable Bob Ojeda gave up four hits and one walk in the first inning, and Houston jumped to a 3-0 lead in their park, the Astrodome. Ojeda settled down after that rocky start, and along with relief pitcher Rick Aguilera, limited the Astros to two hits and no runs through eight innings. Their efforts, though, seemed too little, too late, as Bob Knepper had limited the Mets to two hits and took the 3-0 lead into the ninth inning.

But then the fireworks began exploding! And once again it was Lenny Dykstra who lit the fuse. Lenny led off the ninth for the Mets by lining a pinch-hit triple and scored the Mets' first run on a single by Mookie Wilson. After a ground-out, Keith Hernandez lined a double to the center-field wall, which scored Wilson. That hit narrowed the score to 3-2 and Houston manager Hal Lanier replaced Knepper with his bullpen ace, Dave Smith. Smith, who had saved 33 games during the regular season, walked Gary Carter and then Darryl Strawberry on 3-2 pitches to load the bases. Ray Knight stepped up to the plate and lined a 2-2 pitch to center field, which allowed Keith Hernandez to score the tying run.

Both teams battled tensely through 4 extra innings and then in the top of the 14th inning, the Mets pushed across the go-ahead run. Houston seemed to sag. But in the bottom of the inning, center fielder Billy Hatcher hammered a long home run over the left-field fence and the score was tied again. Neither team scored in the 15th inning, but in the 16th, the Mets erupted for three runs and took a seemingly safe lead into the bottom of the inning. But the Astros answered back with two runs and were actually in position to win the game when Jesse Orosco finally struck out Kevin Bass on a 3-2 pitch to end the longest post-season game in the history of baseball.

After a remarkable game, the Mets had finally won the pennant, and if you ever wondered if major-league ballplayers get nervous, listen to Ray Knight, "I've never been under such pressure. When I came into the dugout after we had tied them in the ninth inning, my legs were shaking." Jesse Orosco, who won 3 games, including the last one, which set a post-season record for relievers, had this to say: "I always get nervous when the bullpen telephone rings and I have to start warming up. Even when we had a 20 game lead during the season, when the phone rang, I got the jitters."

All four teams had provided baseball fans with the jitters as they battled through the most exciting play-offs of all time. Roger Angell, a famous sportswriter, summed it up for everybody when he said, "We've just lived through the greatest week in baseball history."

A lot of people thought that the World Series would seem boring compared to the play-offs but they were wrong. As exciting as the play-offs had been, they turned out to be just a warm-up for the main event.

The same "experts" who had predicted that the Red Sox would wind up fourth or fifth in their division, and then predicted they would easily demolish the Angels, were now saying that Boston didn't have a chance against the mighty Mets.

Sure, the Red Sox had solid hitting and Roger Clemens on the mound, but he wouldn't pitch every day, and they were supposed to be weak on defense and not be able to run well. And because of a new rule, the designated hitter would only be used when the games were played at Boston's Fenway Park. That meant that Don Baylor wouldn't be available, except as a pinch hitter, for the games at Shea Stadium in New York. Baylor is not only one of Boston's best sluggers; he is also a special type of man who supplied the Red Sox with the kind of leadership that turns individuals into a team.

Besides, some people snickered, the Red Sox hadn't won a World Series since 1918 and they almost always found a way to lose the big game.

The Mets, on the other hand, had compiled a regular-season record of 108-54, which matched the best record in the N.L. over the past 77 years! They had solid players at every position, strong reserves, played good defense, and could run. Their pitching staff was deep with starters, four of whom had won 16 or more games, and they had two quality relievers, the left-handed Jesse Orosco and the right-handed Roger McDowell.

So, before a pitch was even thrown, the so-called experts were predicting an easy Mets win. As Boston's manager, John McNamara, joked before the first game, "If we had read the newspapers, we mightn't have shown up."

Even some of the Mets didn't show too much respect for Boston. As Lenny Dykstra said, "I'm not going to say that we have the best team, but they don't run, they don't hit-and-run, and they don't steal bases."

But Bill Buckner, Boston's 36-year-old, sore-legged first baseman, put it all in the proper perspective when he said, "It's been an exciting season and this is a dream match-up. The two best teams in baseball."

If you could have selected a dream pitching match-up for the first game of the World Series, it would have featured Dwight Gooden matching deliveries against Roger Clemens. Gooden had been the dominant pitcher in baseball in 1985 with a 24-4 record and among his many other achievements, he had become the youngest pitcher ever to win the Cy Young Award. The award is given each year to the person who is selected as the best pitcher in his league. Roger Clemens had been just as dominating in 1986 and had also achieved a 24-4 record, which helped him to win the American League Cy Young Award after the season was finished.

But dream match-ups have to wait for pitchers' tired arms, and Dwight and Roger needed another day of rest before they could take to the mound.

So the 55,076 frenzied fans who filled Shea Stadium and the millions of fans watching on television would have to "settle" for a match-up between Boston's Bruce Hurst, who had a 13-8 record during the season, and New York's Ron Darling, who had a 18-6 record.

What the fans got to see was the best-pitched game of the entire series, which the Red Sox eked out with an unearned run in the seventh. The run scored without the Sox even getting a hit! First, Darling walked Jim Rice and then he threw a wild pitch that allowed Rice to reach second base. Then Tim Teufel, who was playing second, let a ground ball hit by Sox catcher Rich Gedman go under his glove and Rice raced home with the only run of the game.

It was a heartbreaking loss for the Mets and especially for Teufel and Darling, who allowed the heavy-hitting Sox only three hits in seven innings while recording eight strike-outs. Although bitterly disappointed, Darling showed a lot of class when he was asked about the error after the game. He just looked at the reporters and said, "Tim didn't want to make the error. He didn't do it on purpose. And that's not what beat us. There hasn't been a team yet that has been shut out and won a game." And, in answering a question about Bruce Hurst, who had pitched four-hit ball and struck out eight Mets in eight innings of work, Ron said, "He just outpitched me."

Before game two began, Billy Joel sang the National Anthem and Elie Wiesel, a famous author and the winner of the 1986 Nobel Peace Prize, threw out the ceremonial first ball.

When the game began, the fans had the match-up that they wanted—Gooden versus Clemens. But the fireworks fizzled because neither Dwight nor Roger had their good stuff. The Boston bats were explosive, however, and they blasted Gooden and three relief pitchers for 18 hits and nine runs.

Dwight's downfall began in the third inning when he walked the first batter, Spike Owens. Clemens attempted to lay down a sacrifice bunt to get Spike into scoring position. But Keith Hernandez charged in toward the plate, scooped up the bunt, and threw to second to get the lead runner. Hernandez is the best-fielding first baseman in the game with nine Golden Glove awards—the most ever by a first baseman—and he makes this play routinely. But this particular time, he threw the ball wildly and both runners were safe. Boggs was up next and he lined a double to left field and the Sox had the lead. Then Marty Barrett and Bill Buckner singled and the Mets were quickly down, 3-0.

The Mets cut the lead to 3-2 in their half of the third but Dwight served up a solo homer to Dave Henderson in the fourth and a two-run homer to Dwight Evans in the fifth. Gooden was removed after the fifth inning, having given up eight hits and six runs (five of them earned). The Mets closed the gap to 6-3 in the bottom of the fifth, which caused McNamara to remove Clemens after four and a third unglamorous innings in which he allowed three runs on five hits, walked four, and struck out only three Mets. The Mets failed to close the gap against relievers Steve Crawford and Bob Stanley, but Boston added three insurance runs and won in a rout, 9-3.

So much for dream match-ups!

The Mets had dug themselves a deep, deep hole and they were stunned. As Ron Darling said, "I never thought that we'd lose two games in our home park to anyone." But they had and now they had to travel to Boston and try to win at least two games at Fenway Park to keep the Series alive.

Although most of the Mets had never played in Fenway and were therefore unfamiliar with The Wall and its other peculiarities, Davey Johnson decided that his team would benefit from a day of rest rather than from a day of practice, so the team did not get a chance to work out before the first game in Fenway.

One Met who did have experience at Fenway was Bob Ojeda, the pitcher who was being called upon to help the Mets gain their first victory. Before he became a Met in the off-season in a deal that moved Calvin Schiraldi to Boston, Bob had spent five years pitching *for* the Red Sox. Opposing him on the mound was Oil Can Boyd, who told reporters before the game that when Ojeda played for Boston, he had told Boyd that he never felt comfortable pitching in Fenway with The Wall behind him.

But it was Boyd who felt uncomfortable after Lenny Dykstra led off the game with a home run. He felt even less comfortable when Backman and Hernandez followed with singles and Carter doubled Backman home. After Strawberry struck out, Ray Knight hit a grounder to Wade Boggs at third. Hernandez was trapped between third and home while Carter lumbered into third. Boston should have tagged at least one of them out, but the rundown was handled like a Three Stooges routine and the Mets wound up with the bases loaded. Danny Heep, batting as the designated hitter, lined a single to center that knocked in Hernandez and Carter and gave the Mets a 4-0 lead. Oil Can had sprung a leak.

Boston rallied for a run in the third inning but stranded two runners as Ojeda struck out Buckner and got Rice to ground into a force-out. That would prove to be the extent of Boston's offense, as Ojeda allowed only 5 hits in seven innings and Roger McDowell finished up with two perfect innings of relief. The Mets, however, had finally begun to hit and punched out 13 hits in a 7-1 victory. Dykstra, with 4 hits, and Gary Carter, with 2 hits and three RBI's, led the Met attack.

Bob Ojeda had faced The Wall and beaten it, and the Mets now trailed by only two games to one.

Ron Darling started the fourth game for the Mets. It was a homecoming for Ron, who had grown up near Boston and who had a lot of friends and family at the game cheering for him. The cheering must have helped because he pitched out of a bases-loaded jam in the first inning and didn't allow any runs in the seven innings that he pitched.

Darling received excellent offensive support from Gary Carter, who hit a two-run homer in the fourth off Red Sox starter Al Nipper and a solo shot in the eighth. Len Dykstra added a two-run shot in the seventh when he hit a fly ball that popped out of Evans's glove and went over the fence in right field. He also received defensive help in the sixth inning from

Mookie Wilson. With Evans on first, Rich Gedman lined a hit off The Wall. Mookie played the bounce perfectly and threw Rich out at second to put the brakes on a Sox rally.

Roger McDowell came on to pitch in the eighth, but had to be rescued after he gave up two runs. Jesse Orosco came in to get the third out and shut down the Sox in the ninth to preserve the Mets' 6-2 victory. New York had evened the Series at 2-2.

Carter, after having a miserable play-off series (4-27), had finally begun to hit with three RBI's in each of the last two games. And, about Lenny Dykstra, who had only eight homers during the regular season, Davey Johnson said, "He has such great concentration now. He's in another zone."

In game five, it was Gooden against Hurst. Gooden escaped a bases-loaded situation in the first inning, but in the second, a triple by Dave Henderson and a sacrifice fly by Spike Owen gave the Sox a 1-0 lead. In the third, after Met shortstop Rafael Santana had booted a grounder, Jim Rice walked and Evans singled, and the Sox led, 2-0. Gooden was knocked out in the fifth when Rice tripled and scored on a soft single to right by Baylor. Sid Fernandez came in and struck out Gedman but the hot-hitting Dave Henderson lashed a double and the Sox led, 4-0. Fernandez shut the Sox out the rest of the way but it was too late. Bruce Hurst made the four-run lead stand up as he surrendered just two runs to the Mets, an eighth-inning homer by Tim Teufel, and another in the ninth when, with two out, Wilson doubled and Santana singled. Then Hurst struck out Len Dykstra to end the game.

The "invincible" Mets limped back to Shea stadium knowing that they had to win the next two games. They were one loss away from having their glorious season end in bitter disappointment.

Game six was, at the least, one of the most exciting games in World Series history, one that the 55,078 fans in Shea Stadium and the millions of people who watched it on TV will always remember.

The game didn't need any extra excitement, but it got some from an unexpected source in the first inning when a man with a yellow parachute dropped out of the nighttime sky and landed in the infield. Attached to the parachute was a sign reading, "Let's Go Mets."

But it was Boston that got going in the very first inning as Dwight Evans hit a two-out double to score Wade Boggs. They added another run in the second on consecutive singles by Owens, Boggs, and Barrett. Clemens had been breezing along, but the Mets broke up his no-hitter and his shutout in the fifth when, after Strawberry had walked and stolen second, Ray Knight singled him home. Wilson singled Knight to third as Evans bobbled the ball in right field and he scored the tying run while Danny Heep was grounding into a double play.

Roger McDowell pitched for the Mets in the seventh inning and began by walking Marty Barrett. After a ground-out, Ray Knight threw wildly on Rice's grounder and the Sox had runners on first and third. Barrett scored to make it 3-2 and Rice moved to second as Evans grounded out. Next, Rich Gedman lined a single to left and Jim Rice headed home, but Mookie Wilson made a beautiful throw and Gary Carter blocked the plate, making a quick tag to nab Rice at the plate for the third out.

The Mets managed to tie the game in the eighth off reliever Calvin Schiraldi when Gary Carter hit a sacrifice fly to score Lee Mazzilli. Lee had started the inning by delivering a clutch pinch-hit single.

Neither team scored in the ninth, and the fans and players felt the tension build as the game went into extra innings. Dave Henderson, who had been the big hero in Boston's comeback win against California in game five, rose to the occasion once again in the tenth and smacked a home run off Rick Aguilera. They added another run when, with two outs, Boggs doubled and Barrett singled him home with his record-tying 13th hit of the Series.

The Mets' whole season was hanging by a very thin thread, and the thread got thinner as ex-Met Calvin Schiraldi retired the first two batters. There was one out left to the Mets' season. Gary Carter was the New York batter and he looked into the Red Sox dugout. "I saw them excited, getting ready to run off the field and celebrate. I didn't want to be the last out and have to think about it until spring training." Carter singled. Rookie Kevin Mitchell came up to pinch-hit and thought, *I'm not ready to go home*. Mitchell singled.

Ray Knight was the batter as the fans began chanting, "Let's Go, Mets." Knight stood in the batter's box and remembered his grandfather's saying, "If you have grit, all things are possible." With two strikes against him, Knight delivered a single and Carter scored as Mitchell went to third. But the Sox still led 5-4 as Bob Stanley was brought in to pitch to Mookie Wilson. Mookie walked up to the plate telling himself, "Do not strike out! Please give yourself a chance. Hit the ball." The count went to 2-2 and once more, the Mets were down to their final strike. The tension rose steadily as Mookie fouled off two pitches. Stanley pitched again; it was a wild pitch and as Ray Knight took second, Kevin Mitchell raced home with the tying run. The tension rose more as Mookie fouled off two more pitches. On the next pitch, he hit a bouncer toward Bill Buckner at first. But the ball went under Buckner's glove and Ray Knight came home with the winning run. The Mets were still alive!

The fans at Shea cheered and the Mets danced with delight. An excited Keith Hernandez shouted, "It is one of the greatest comebacks in the history of baseball!" It was, in fact, the only time in the history of the World Series that a team had been down by two runs in extra innings and had come back to win.

The Red Sox were stunned. After the game, Buckner told reporters, "I saw the ball well. It bounced and it bounced and then it didn't bounce. It just skipped. I don't remember the last time I missed a ball like that, but I'll remember that one."

A capacity crowd of 55,032 fans rocked Shea Stadium as game seven got underway. Tens of millions more watched on TV sets all across America. Baseball fever had gripped the country.

If anyone thought that Boston would roll over after their heartbreaking loss in game six, those thoughts quickly disappeared when the Sox erupted for three runs in the second inning off Ron Darling. First, Evans and Gedman hit back-to-back homers and then Boggs singled home Dave Henderson.

The Mets had to climb out of yet another hole. Sid Fernandez relieved Darling with one out in the fourth and held the Sox in check through the sixth. In the bottom of the sixth, Lee Mazzilli pinch-hit for Fernandez and delivered a single against Bruce Hurst. Mookie Wilson followed with a single and Teufel walked to load the bases. Keith Hernandez lined a long single to left center and two runs scored. Carter followed with a sacrifice fly that evened the score at 3-3. The Mets' Magic had struck again and Shea Stadium echoed with the roar of their fans.

Ray Knight led off the seventh inning with a home run off Schiraldi to give the Mets the lead for the first time in the game. Dykstra followed with a single and a steal of second. Santana singled Dykstra home and McDowell sacrificed Santana to second. Joe Sambito came in to pitch, and he gave up two walks and a sacrifice fly to Keith Hernandez, and the Mets led, 6-3.

The Sox came right back, though, and scored two runs in the eighth off McDowell as Buckner and Rice singled and Evans doubled them home with a blast to left center. Orosco replaced McDowell and closed out the inning.

The Mets bounced back with two runs of their own in their half of the eighth, one of which was a home run by Darryl Strawberry.

Orosco retired three straight in the ninth inning, and the World Series was finally over. The Red Sox and the Mets had given the baseball fans of America the kind of excitement that they could treasure forever. It had been a wonderful World Series!

CHAPTER 5

Sweet Music

There were, as has come to be usual, no repeat winners and plenty of surprises in the divisional races in 1987. In the N.L. East the St. Louis Cardinals played leapfrog with the Mets and reclaimed the title that they had lost to the New Yorkers in 1986. In the West the San Francisco Giants, who had lost one hundred games just two years earlier, were the surprise winners over the Reds and the Astros, who in one year went from being a division winner to a third-place finisher 14 games off the pace.

In the American League the Detroit Tigers took the East in exciting fashion. Going into the final weekend of the season, they trailed Toronto by a game, but they swept the three-game series, including a 1-0 thriller on the last day, to win the division by two games. The defending champion Red Sox tumbled to a fifth-place finish, 20 games behind the Tigers.

The unheralded Minnesota Twins, who won the West, provided the biggest surprise. They went from being a sixth-place team that had lost 92 games in 1986 to easing into the division championship two games in front of the Royals. The California Angels, the previous year's winner, switched places with the Twins and sank into sixth place, 10 games behind.

The Cardinals had beaten back determined challenges from both the Mets and the Expos despite not having Jack Clark's big bat available down the stretch. Clark had hammered out 35 home runs and knocked in 106 runs, including 15 game winners, before he went down with an ankle injury in early September. He had supplied the Cards with their only real crunch, and without his bat in the lineup it was as though someone had pulled the plug on their power supply.

Without Clark in the lineup the Cards would have to rely on their other assets: speed, defense, and pitching. When you mention speed, you start with their leadoff hitter, left fielder Vince Coleman. Coleman had stolen 109 bases during the season and had become the first player ever to steal 100 or more bases in each of his first three seasons. Coleman was the main man, but almost everybody on the team ran. That puts a lot of pressure on a pitcher, who can't concentrate solely on the batter.

The left side of the infield was anchored by two Gold Glove winners, shortstop Ozzie Smith and third sacker Terry Pendleton. And with the speed of Coleman in left and Willie McGee in center, Manager

Whitey Herzog didn't have to worry too much about balls dropping safely in the outfield.

John Tudor and Danny Cox were the mainstays of the starting rotation, and Todd Worrell, with 33 saves, and Ken Dayley were the closers.

The Giants, under the patient tutoring of Manager Roger Craig and the shrewd trading of President Al Rosen, had undergone a dramatic transformation in just two seasons. They had gone from a doormat to a division championship and were hoping to bring San Francisco its first pennant in 25 years. The Giants could run, but unlike the Cards they relied on a power game to score runs. They had whacked 205 home runs, second best in the National League, and every starter on their team with the exception of shortstop Jose Uribe had hit at least 10 home runs. Their biggest thumpers were first baseman Will Clark with 35 round trippers, third baseman Kevin Mitchell (22), and outfielders Chili Davis (24), Candy Maldonado (20), and Jeffrey Leonard (19).

On the morning of the first game the Cards had to deal with another injury. Danny Cox, the scheduled starting pitcher, woke up with a stiff neck and was unable to pitch. Cards' Manager Whitey Herzog stayed calm, handed the ball to rookie Greg Matthews, and told him to do his best. All Matthews did was pitch four-hit ball for seven and two-thirds innings and single in the two final runs in a 5-3 win.

Dave Dravecky helped even the series the next day when he shut out the Cards on a sparkling two-hitter as the Giants won 5-0. Will Clark got the Giants rolling when he stroked a two-run homer off Cards' ace John Tudor. Tudor, who hadn't lost a game since August 16, also gave up a towering home run to Jeffrey Leonard, his second in two games. Leonard, who has five home-run trots, circled the bases very slowly, with his left hand pinned to his side—or as he put it, "left flap down." Leonard slowed his trot to a walk between third and home and just smiled as the fans in Busch Stadium showered him with jeers.

The scene shifted to Candlestick Park, San Francisco, but Leonard kept his act intact by blasting his third home run in three games. The Giants, who led 4-0 and had the bases loaded in the fifth inning, were about to break the game wide open. But reliever Bob Forsch choked off the rally, and "that," said Herzog, "was the turning point."

When the Cards came to bat, Jim Lindeman, subbing at first base for Jack Clark, smacked a two-run homer. "That really picked us up," said center fielder Willie McGee. "We hadn't scored in 16 innings." One inning later the Cards stroked five consecutive singles and added in a sacrifice fly to score four runs, and they held on to win the game 6-5. Afterward, Leonard gave his view of the game. "One lousy inning again. You know, it was a typical Cardinal inning, too—singles."

The Giants evened the series the next day with a 4-2 win, and Mr. Leonard hit another home run, making him the first player ever to hit home runs in four consecutive play-off games. After the game Roger

Craig said, "I don't know what Jeffrey's feeding on these days, but I'm going to find out and feed it to the whole team."

The Giants took the pivotal fifth game 6-3 using Cardinal tactics—four stolen bases and outstanding relief pitching—and headed back to St. Louis needing only one victory in the remaining two games to grab the pennant. But they came up empty as the Cards dealt them consecutive shutouts, 1-0 in game six and 6-0 in game seven. John Tudor, with relief help from Todd Worrell and Ken Dayley, took care of the pitching, and Tony Pena scored the only run of the sixth game on a sacrifice fly by Jose Oquendo. Danny Cox, who enhanced his reputation as a big-game pitcher, took care of the pitching in game seven, and he received all the offensive help he needed in the second inning when the Cards erupted for four runs, including a three-run homer by super-sub Oquendo.

The scrappy Cardinals overcame injuries to key players and a record-setting performance by Jeffrey Leonard to win their second pennant in three years. They bunched their singles, strung their runs together, got clutch performances from reserves, and played superb defense. And their pitching turned the powerful Giant bats into toothpicks by holding them scoreless over the final 22 innings.

It was on to the World Series.

The Tigers were heavy favorites to defeat the Twins in the American League Championship Series.

Detroit had posted a 98-64 record, the best in baseball, and had closed with a surge by sweeping Toronto. Their manager, Sparky Anderson, said that this team was stronger than the 1984 team that had won the World Series.

Detroit had powerful hitting led by shortstop Alan Trammell, who had driven in 105 runs while whacking 28 homers and hitting .343. And he had plenty of support from sluggers like first baseman Darrell Evans (34 homers, 99 RBI's); left fielder Kirk Gibson (24 homers); and rookie catcher Matt Nokes (32 homers, 87 RBI's). As a team they had hit a major-league-leading 225 dingers.

Detroit also had strong starting pitching anchored by Jack Morris and Doyle Alexander, a late-season addition to the staff who had reeled off nine straight victories; Walt Terrell, who almost never lost in Tiger Stadium, and veteran Frank Tanana completed the rotation.

The Twins had played like Dr. Jekyll and Mr. Hyde. At home, in the Metrodome, they had played almost as efficiently as the machines that controlled the temperature in the stadium, and they had compiled the best record (56-25) of any team in either league. ever recorded by a first-place team.

The Twins had played like Dr. Jeckyll and Mr. Hyde. At home, in the Metrodome, they had played almost as efficiently as the machines that controlled the temperature in the stadium, and they had compiled the best record (56-25) of any team in either league.

But their road record (29-52) had been the third worst in the A.L. and the worst ever by a division champion.

Tom Brunansky, the Twins' hard-hitting right fielder, acknowledged the importance of the Metrodome and the realization that the Tigers had beaten them in the season series when he said, "I think everybody on this club wants to win these first two games at home. Before the series begins, it's on our minds that we'll need our home-field advantage." Two other points may have been on the Twins' minds too: Their two best starting pitchers, Frank Viola and Bert Blyleven, hadn't beaten the Tigers all year; and Detroit had even taken four of the six games that the teams had played at the Metrodome.

The Twins, though, weren't lacking in firepower. They had a lot of heavy hitters, such as Kent Hrbek (34 homers, 90 RBI's); Gary Gaetti (31, 109); Kirby Puckett (28, 99, with a .332 average); and Brunansky (32, 85). They had also added Jeff Reardon to their bullpen. Reardon, who had had 31 saves, is known as the Terminator for the way he finishes games.

Now the Twins were going to try to finish off the Tigers, and as Gaetti said, "They ended the season with a better record than us, but no one can see the future."

If Gaetti could have seen the future, he would have seen that he smacked two home runs off Doyle Alexander and that the Twins took the first game 8-5.

In the second game Blyleven and Juan Berenguer, who was outstanding, outpitched Jack Morris, who had brought a 12-0 career record against the Twins into the game. The key hit in the 6-3 win was a two-run double by Tim Laudner, the weak-hitting catcher. The Metrodome crowd roared with delight and waved their large handkerchiefs.

Because the Metrodome is enclosed, the crowd noise can be almost deafening and certainly distracting for visiting teams. But Morris loved it. "That was the most amazing crowd I've been in front of in my life. I enjoyed every second of it even though they weren't rooting for me. That's what this game is all about."

After the second game there seemed to be a subtle shift of feeling between the teams. A drop of doubt seemed to seep into the Tiger players. "I don't think we're ready to concede at this point," observed Kirk Gibson. "But we're not in the best of positions."

The Twins began to believe that they could really take it. "The ball is in our court," said Blyleven. "I think we'll win it in Detroit."

The third game, played in Tiger Stadium, quickly turned into a slugfest as Detroit erupted for five runs in the third inning. But the Twins battled back behind home runs by shortstop Greg Gagne and Brunansky and took a 6-5 lead in the seventh when Gaetti knocked in two runs.

The Twins needed six outs and brought Reardon in to finish off the Tigers. But Pat Sheridan, who hadn't hit a homer since August or driven in a run since early September, totaled the Terminator with a two-run homer to give the Tigers a 7-6 thriller. Even after the tough loss Gaetti appreciated the sheer excitement of playing for a championship. "This has been a great series. It's more fun than I imagined."

In game four the Twins got homers from Puckett and Gagne and led 4-2 going into the sixth. The Tigers, though, cut the lead to 4-3 and had runners on second and third with only one out. "We were in big trouble," Gaetti noted. "And we had to do something to get us out." Laudner again did the big something; he picked the runner off third and the Twins took the game 5-3.

The Twins came out thumping early in game five as they rocked Alexander for four runs in the second inning. The Tigers closed the gap to 4-3, but the Twins were relentless and pounded out a 9-5 win to capture their first pennant since 1965.

In the happy clubhouse after the game, Gaetti, who had been named the MVP, walked over to Brunansky with the trophy and said, "You deserve this." Then they just hugged each other and Gaetti added, "I don't think about awards. I just think about winning. This isn't an individual effort. This is 25 guys."

Brunansky echoed his teammate by saying, "We played like a team."

And Detroit's top reliever, Mike Henneman, summed it all up. "They didn't give us a chance to regroup. Whenever we made a mistake, they cashed in. This wasn't the same Minnesota team I faced all year."

The Cardinals' chances were dealt a serious blow when they learned that third baseman Terry Pendleton, a Gold Glove winner and their second-leading power hitter, had to be scratched. Herzog responded with his usual aplomb, "I don't like injuries, but there's not a lot you can do about them, so there's no use fretting about them."

Herzog, however, had a lot to fret about in the fourth inning of game one as the home-field Twins erupted like a volcano and sent seven runs spewing across the plate to take a 7-1 lead. Since the rules call for playing nine innings, they had to finish the game, but as Whitey Herzog said, "We were not going to score seven runs off Viola." "Sweet Music" was into his rhythm, allowing only five hits in eight innings of work. Early in the game Viola used his change-up, and his second time through the Cardinal lineup he used his 90-MPH heater. By the time the Cards came up for their third go-around, they didn't know what to expect and were completely off balance. As Viola said, "I felt I was totally in control of the game."

Gaetti began the fourth inning with a single and came in to score the Twins' first run on a single by Brunansky. They scored the next four runs in a bunch as left fielder Dan Gladden ripped a hanging curve over the wall in left center for the first World Series grand slam since 1970. The Twins' fans stood and waved their Homer Hankies and thundered a roar that was measured at 118 decibels, or about the same level of noise that you would experience if you stood a few hundred feet away from a jet plane on takeoff.

The Twins padded their score with a two-run homer by Steve Lombardozzi and an RBI double by Gladden to waltz away with a 10-1 win.

Gaetti got things going again in the second game by lining a 400-foot homer into the left-field seats off Danny Cox in the second inning. In the fourth inning, like Old Faithful, the Twins erupted again—this time for six runs. The inning began quietly enough, with a ground out, but then Puckett and Hrbek each lined singles to right, and Gaetti walked to load the bases. DH Randy Bush lashed a double to the wall to knock in two runs, and then Cox gave Brunansky an intentional walk to reload the bases. Cox seemed to have contained the damage as he got Lombardozzi on a short fly for the second out, but Laudner came through with another clutch hit, which scored Gaetti and Bush, who made a head-first slide and touched the plate with his left hand an instant before Pena slapped the tag on him. Gladden singled to drive in the Twins' sixth run and knock Cox out of the game. Gagne added a run-scoring double to give them a 7-0 lead.

Blyleven, who had pitched perfectly for four inning, gave up a single run in the fifth. After Laudner's long homer upped the score to 8-1 in the sixth, the Cards scratched out a second run off Blyleven in the seventh and two more off Berenguer in the eighth. But the Terminator came in to tame the Cards in the ninth as the Twins took the game 8-4 and the Series lead 2-0.

The Twins, though, didn't suffer from overconfidence. "The Cardinals are a good team," noted Kirby Puckett, "and they can run themselves back into a game real quick."

While the teams moved to St. Louis for the next three games, New York Yankee owner George Steinbrenner stole the headlines by announcing that Billy Martin would be back for his fifth term as Yankee manager. As soon as the announcement was made, fans began guessing about how long it would take for Martin to be fired again.

The temperature at game time was a cool 49 degrees, and the hitters on both teams were even colder. The Twins finally eked out a run in the sixth when Tudor walked two batters and Brunansky looped a single to right. Twins' Manager Tom Kelly decided to replace Les Straker, who had pitched shutout ball for six innings, with Berenguer. Oquendo lashed a single to center on Berenguer's first pitch, and Pena followed by punching a single to right. Pendleton, pinch-hitting for Tudor, moved the runners up with a perfect sacrifice bunt, and then the slumping Vince Coleman skimmed a double down the third-base line to give the Cards a 2-1 lead. Coleman stole third on the next pitch and came in to score the final run of the game on Ozzie Smith's single.

Game four took a surprising turn in the fourth inning after the teams had exchanged runs in the third. Pena got things going with a single, and Oquendo singled to right. The next batter was Tom Lawless, filling in for the injured Terry Pendleton. Lawless had gotten two hits during the 1987 season in 25 at bats for a batting average that required a microscope to be seen. In his first at bat Viola had struck him out—looking. But this time he found a pitch to his liking, drilled it out to left field, and watched as the second home run of his major-league career cleared the wall. He broke into the type of slow trot that Jeffrey Leonard would have enjoyed as he became only the fourth non-pitcher in World Series history to hit a home run without having hit one during the season. Before the Twins, and everyone else, recovered from the shock, the Cards added three more runs and took a commanding 7-1 lead.

The Twins tried to come back, but great defense and solid pitching stymied them. In the fifth they had runners on first and third with one out when Gaetti hit a smash between short and third. Ozzie dove to his right to make the stop and, while on his knees, threw to second for the force-out. Brunansky then lashed a sinking liner to left that Coleman dove for and caught with a head-first slide.

The Twins, trailing 7-2, made another run at the Cards in the seventh, but Ken Dayley came in and, with the bases loaded, struck out Gaetti and got Brunansky on a foul pop to preserve the win and even the Series at two games each.

In game five the Cards broke a scoreless duel in the sixth inning after they had run themselves out of two earlier opportunities. Coleman got them going with an infield single that handcuffed Hrbek at first. Ozzie then laid down a bunt between the mound and third base that Blyleven couldn't pick up, and the Cards had their two best base runners on. After Herr struck out, Coleman and Smith pulled a double steal, and Kelly decided to walk Driessen and try for the double play. The Twins took a small breath as Willie McGee struck out, but their hope turned to despair as Curt Ford lined a Blyleven fastball up the middle to give St. Louis a 2-0 lead. The Cards added another run after an error by Greg Gagne, which meant that they had scored three runs while hitting only one ball out of the infield. One inning later they manufactured another run when Coleman walked, took second on a balk, stole third, and came home on an infield single by Smith. "They're pretty much like a bunch of gnats swirling around you," observed Gaetti.

In the eighth Gaetti tagged Todd Worrell for a two-out, two-run triple that McGee caught up with but dropped as he crashed into the wall. The Twins threatened again in the ninth and had the tying runs on base, but Worrell got Don Baylor to pop up and end the game. The Cards had reshuffled the deck and now needed only one more win to capture the World Series.

The Twins, as they had been all season, were a flop on the road. After scoring 18 runs in two games at the Metrodome, they had managed to score only five runs in the three games at Busch Stadium. As Gaetti put it, "I'm glad to get out of here."

But waiting for them at home was an unfavorable pitching match-up—Cardinal ace John Tudor against rookie Les Straker. And the Cards also had their running game in gear, with eight steals in the last three games, and this seemed to rattle the Twins. But Herzog wasn't convinced that running would be a significant factor in the smaller dimensions of the Metrodome. "They've got guys who hit home runs. We can steal six bases and still lose 5-4."

It was the Cards, though, who got on the scoreboard first as they took a 5-2 lead into the bottom of the fifth inning. But then the Twins brought out the big bats and battered the Cards. Gaetti knocked in a run with a double to left, and the next batter, Don Baylor, crashed a change-up into the left-field seats. After Brunansky singled, Ricky Horton took over for Tudor. A groundout moved Brunansky to second, and a single brought him home with the fourth run of the inning to give the Twins a 6-5 lead.

"It happened so quickly," said Herzog. "It was bang-bang."

In the next inning Kent Hrbek iced the game when he went bang-bang on a Ken Dayley pitch with the bases loaded and gave the Twins a 10-5 lead on their way to an 11-5 victory. "I wish I could have run around the bases twice," said the Minnesota native. "I can't tell you how big a thrill it is with your friends and family in the stands."

The season, as it often does, had come down to one decisive game. And the Twins had their ace, Viola, to play against the Cards, while St. Louis had to rely on rookie Joe Magrane. It was the Cards, though, who struck first as consecutive singles in the second inning by Lindeman, McGee, and Pena produced a 1-0 lead. Manager Tom Kelly rushed Blyleven to the bullpen. "Another hit or two and Frank was out of there." Steve Lake got the fourth hit of the inning to drive in McGee, but then "Sweet Music" Viola closed the case on the Cards. When he came into the dugout he announced, "That's all they're getting. That's it." And he delivered on his promise as he retired ten straight batters and held St. Louis to only two hits in the next six innings.

The Twins, in the meantime, picked up a run in the bottom of the second with the help of a hit batsman and three singles. The Cards avoided more damage when Coleman threw out Baylor in the middle of the rally when he tried to score from second on a single.

In the fifth Gagne was given credit for an infield hit when the first-base umpire ruled that he had beaten Magrane to the bag. Herzog decided to bring in Cox despite the fact that Magrane was pitching a strong game and that Cox had never before pitched with only two days' rest. The strategy backfired as Kirby Puckett smoked Cox's first pitch for a double into right center that sent Gagne racing home with the tying run. And only great defense by the Cards prevented the Twins from grabbing the lead. First, catcher Steve Lake threw Puckett out at third when he tried to move up on a wild pitch. Then, with Gaetti on second Baylor singled to left. Coleman fielded the ball and fired a strike to Lake, who made the tag and held on to the ball despite the ferocious collision that resulted when Gaetti barreled into him. So despite two singles, a double, and a walk, the Twins only scored the one run.

In the sixth inning Cox walked the first two batters he faced and was replaced by Worrell. Worrell got one out, walked the next batter to load the bases, and then K'd Gladden for the second out. Gagne was up next, and he hit a two-hop bouncer down the third-base line. Lawless made a diving grab for the ball, but his throw was too late to catch the speedy Gagne, and the Twins had the lead, 3-2.

The Twins added another run in the eighth on an RBI double by Gladden, and in the ninth the Terminator replaced Viola and finished off the Cards 1-2-3 to preserve the 4-2 win. The Twins had dreamed the impossible dream and they had made it come true.

After the game "Sweet Music," who was named the MVP, was asked if he minded coming out of the game after setting down St. Louis in order in the eighth. "No. This is a team game," he shot back. "We've won that way all year."

A happy Steve Lombardozzi knew what it all meant. "We're no longer the Twinkies. We're the World Champion Minnesota Twins."

CHAPTER 6

A Team of Destiny

There wasn't a lot of suspense in the divisional races in 1988, as three of the four contests were decided pretty early. But there were, as usual, lots of surprises.

In the American League, the Boston Red Sox provided both surprise and suspense, as they bounced back from a fifth-place finish in 1987 to capture the Eastern Division title on the last weekend of the season. And the Oakland Athletics, who hadn't had a winning season since 1981, steamrolled their way through the league and won the West with ease.

Over in the National League, the New York Mets, to no one's great surprise, dominated the Eastern Division for the second time in three years, while in the West, the Los Angeles Dodgers, who were coming off two consecutive losing seasons, defied all expectations in winning their division.

The A's had clearly demonstrated that they were the dominant team in the AL. Combining power hitting with strong pitching and solid defense, the A's won 104 games, the best in the majors, and outdist-anced the second place Twins by 13 games.

The main basher on the A's was right fielder Jose Canseco, who had led both leagues with 42 home runs and 124 RBI's, becoming the first player in history to hit 40 or more homers and steal 40 or more bases. Canseco and first baseman Mark McGwire, who hammered out 32 homers and knocked in 99 runs, were nicknamed the Bash Brothers both because of their slugging and the way they celebrated their home runs by bashing their forearms together. Center fielder Dave Henderson, who smacked 24 dingers while driving in 94 runs, also wielded a big bat. And Rookie of the Year Walt Weiss, who hadn't made an error since the All-Star game, was a human vacuum cleaner at shortstop. Dave Stewart, with a 21-12 record, led a staff of starting pitchers that also included 17-game-winner Bob Welch and 16-game-winner Storm Davis. Manager Tony LaRussa also had a strong and versatile bullpen crew that was anchored by Dennis Eckersley, who had led the majors with 45 saves.

But despite the fact that the A's had ridden rough-shod over the league while Boston had limped home like a lame nag, and despite the fact that the A's had taken nine of the 12 meetings between the teams, Boston was given a good chance of derailing Oakland's ride to the World Series.

The Red Sox, as usual, were loaded offensively. Wade Boggs had won his fourth consecutive batting title with a major-league-leading .366 average, and left fielder Mike Greenwell and center fielder Ellis Burks had blossomed into All-Stars while Jody Reed had taken over at shortstop during the season and added even more punch to the Boston attack. And Boston not only scored runs in bunches, they also had two of the best starting pitchers in baseball, Roger Clemens and left-hander Bruce Hurst, as well as a bullpen stopper in Lee Smith.

But the A's kept themselves on the right track in game one of the ALCS as Jose Canseco flexed his muscles in the top of the first inning and ripped a Bruce Hurst fastball over the Green Monster in left field. The Red Sox threatened in the second inning, but Walt Weiss saved a run with a spectacular diving stop, and then, with the bases loaded, Dave Stewart fanned Wade Boggs to close out the inning.

After the Red Sox tied the game in the seventh on a bases-loaded sacrifice fly by Boggs, the A's retook the lead in the eighth 2-1. But Boston did not go quietly. With two down in the ninth, Reed ripped a double off Eckersley, Rich Gedman drew a base on balls, and Boggs stepped up to bat. Eckersley came with his heat, nicking the outside corner for two quick strikes. Eckersley's third pitch was a low inside sinker that Boggs fouled off. Then Eckersley fooled Boggs with a high fastball. "He changed zones on me. I was looking for a low sinker." Boggs swung and missed, and the game was over.

A relieved Tony LaRussa, realizing that Boggs had struck out only 34 times in 719 plate appearances during the season, sighed, "I hope that's the last time we have to face that situation. It's a tough way to beat the Red Sox." But Eckersley, displaying the confidence that is required of a late-inning reliever who is on the mound only when the game is on the line, loved it. "That is where I want to be, right there."

In game two Roger Clemens and Storm Davis were locked in a no-run pitchers' duel until the sixth inning, when Dave Henderson dropped a two-out liner that allowed the Red Sox to score two unearned runs. With Boston breezing along behind Clemens, it looked like the A's express was going to get flagged down. "I thought we were a shoo-in," said Sox manager Joe Morgan. "The way Roger was throwing the ball, I figured no way they do it."

But in the very next inning, they did it. Henderson, hoping to make up for his fielding lapse, got things started with a single, and then Canseco lifted an 0-2 fastball over the screen in left to tie the score at 2-2. And two outs later Mark McGwire put the A's in the lead by singling in Carney Lansford. The Sox managed to tie the game in the seventh when Rich Gedman stroked a home run, but the A's pulled it out in the ninth when Walt Weiss singled home the winning run in the top of the inning off Lee Smith, while Eckersley earned another save by setting down the Sox in order in the bottom of the inning.

The A's had trumped Boston's two aces at Fenway, and with the ALCS moving to Oakland, where the Sox were 0-6 in 1988 and 1-14 in their last 15 games, it didn't take a weatherman to see which way the wind was blowing. Canseco, though, put a wet finger in the air anyway and announced, "At most, I see it going three more games."

And even though Boston began game three with a barrage, and led 5-0 after only an inning and a half, the A's bounced right back in the bottom of the second. McGwire got things going with a dinger over the wall in left, and after Weiss doubled in a run, Lansford ripped a two-run homer that narrowed the A's deficit to 5-4. One inning later McGwire legged out a two-out single, and catcher Ron Hassey followed with a smash into the right-field stands to give the A's a 6-5 lead. And the Athletics never looked back, pounding out a 10-6 win. Gene Nelson picked up his second successive win in relief, and Eckersley closed out the game with two perfect innings to earn his third consecutive save, establishing a new ALCS record.

Canseco got the scoring started in the first inning of game four with his third homer of the ALCS, tying a record that George Brett had set in 1978 and equaled in 1985. And in the eighth inning, with the A's leading by only a 2-1 score, Canseco ignited a two-run rally with a single and a steal of second. Then Eckersley came out of the bullpen, shutting the door on Boston's season and securing the American League pennant for the Oakland A's.

In the winners' clubhouse the cocky A's were sounding very confident. "We took the 3-0 lead in games and wanted to end it," announced Carney Lansford. "This team has the killer instinct." And they seemed to prove it with their sweep—the first 4-0 sweep in a championship series since the Reds swept the Yankees in the 1976 World Series.

"The Mets and Dodgers have watched these games and they can see what we've done, so they know it's going to be a tough task," proclaimed Mark McGwire. "We just do everything to get the victory." And the other Bash Brother also threw down a challenge to the senior circuit. "We're going to be the team to beat," said Canseco. "We have the better record; the pressure will be on our opponent."

The match-up between the Mets and the Dodgers seemed like a mismatch. The Mets, the only team in the National League to win 100 games, had led the league in homers and runs scored; their defense had made the fewest errors, and their pitching staff had allowed the fewest earned runs. They were a power-house who seemed to have a star at every position, and they were coming into the NLCS with a full head of steam, having won 19 of their final 22 games. And they were confident of their ability to beat the Dodgers, something they had done ten times in their 11 meetings during the season.

When most people looked at the Dodger lineup, they saw Kirk Gibson, Orel Hershiser, and a lot of nameless role players who would be lucky to warm the Mets' bench. But while it was obvious that Gibson and Hershiser were the main men in L.A.'s rise to the top in the West, it was also true that they wouldn't have risen very high without solid support from their slugging right fielder Mike Marshall, second baseman Steve Sax, who keyed their running game, and catcher Mike Scioscia. Another key in L.A.'s rise to first place had involved the crafting of a formidable pitching staff out of a group of castoffs like starters Tim Belcher and Tim Leary and ace reliever Jay Howell. But there was no denying the fact that Gibson and Hershiser shone so brightly that their teammates seemed to stand in the shadows.

Gibson had made his presence felt from the first day he put on a Dodger uniform. Even in spring training he showed his new teammates the intensity and determination that had been the hallmark of his career in Detroit. He had supplied the Dodgers with home-run power and speed on the bases, but even more importantly he had given them the will to win. But when the Dodgers clashed with the Mets, the ex-Tiger performed as if he had no claws. In the ten games that he had played against the Mets, he was 8-for-36 with 19 strikeouts and only one home run, which was, incredibly, half of the Dodgers' 1988 team total against the Mets' pitching staff. Further complicating matters for Gibson and the Dodgers was the fact that the fleet left fielder was hurting, his mobility limited by a pull in his left hamstring. But when questioned about his availability, Gibson demonstrated his toughness and his team spirit. "I'll be playing tomorrow. It doesn't matter how it feels. My teammates are counting on me being out there and making things happen."

Orel Hershiser, the other cornerstone player for the Dodgers, had ended a fabulous season in sensational style by pitching six straight shutouts and compiling a record-setting streak of 59 consecutive scoreless innings. Nicknamed "Bulldog" by Lasorda, Hershiser had sunk his teeth into National League hitters and bitten off 23 wins. The Dodgers' dependence on Hershiser was so great that most observers considered his performance in game one of the NLCS to be the key to the Dodgers' limited chances of success against the heavily favored Mets. "If the Mets win the first game, it could be over in five," suggested St. Louis manager Whitey Herzog.

Orel was also aware of the game's potential importance. "It's an attitude-adjustment game. The Mets won ten of eleven from us, and if they win, they'll be continuing their dominance. But if we can beat the Mets, then things will have changed. But," warned Hershiser, showing the fierce determination that had infused the team, "even if we lose, the Dodgers won't quit. We'll fight back."

But as game one entered the ninth inning, it was the Mets who were forced to fight back. The Dodgers had nicked Dwight Gooden, who had begun the game with a 4-0 lifetime record and a near-invisible 0.34 ERA at Dodger Stadium, for single runs in the first and seventh innings. And Hershiser, who was continuing to weave his web of invincibility, was only three outs away from his seventh straight shutout. But the

Mets, having won 19 games in their last at-bat during the season, were no strangers to late-inning heroics.

Greg Jeffries, their rookie phenom, opened the ninth with a single to center, his third hit of the night and the Mets' sixth. After a groundout moved Jeffries to second, Darryl Strawberry stepped into the batter's box. Hershiser had kept the NL's top slugger off balance in his three previous trips to the plate, but on his fourth try the Straw Man lashed a double into the alley in right center, knocking in Jeffries with the first run scored off Hershiser in 67$\frac{1}{3}$ innings. Lasorda, thinking that Hershiser would sag after finally giving up a run, brought in Jay Howell, his bullpen stopper, to close out the game. Howell walked Kevin McReynolds to put the potential lead run on base, but fanned Howard Johnson for the second out. Relying on his curve ball, Howell got two quick strikes on the next batter, Gary Carter. Howell's third pitch was another sweeping curve, low and away from the right-handed hitter, but Carter managed to get the end of his bat on the ball and send a looping fly into short center field. As John Shelby raced in to make the catch, Strawberry and McReynolds flashed around the bases. With the ball falling toward the ground, Shelby lunged for it and briefly snared it in his glove before he hit the ground and jarred the ball loose. The Mets, who had been down to their last strike, now led 3-2, and Randy Myers, their flame-throwing bullpen ace, pitched a perfect ninth inning as the New Yorkers completed a stunning come-from-behind win. Hershiser tried to minimize what had been a heartbreaking defeat. "It's only one game. It's a tough defeat, yes. But it's just one loss." But Gibson spoke what most of the team was feeling, "It was as tough a loss as I've had to swallow in my professional career." While Keith Hernandez, looking at the situation from the winner's clubhouse, expressed the Mets' reaction, "Obviously, this is a big win for us and a big loss for them. This puts us in the position of putting the hammer on them."

And the Dodgers could have come out really flat and ready to be hit. But David Cone, the Mets starting pitcher in game two, picked them up and got their juices flowing. Cone was writing a column for a New York newspaper during the NLCS, and after game one he had sounded off with some negative comments about a few of the Dodgers. He was especially nasty toward Jay Howell. "This is the Dodgers' idea of a stopper? Seeing Howell and his curveball reminded us of a high school pitcher."

Tommy Lasorda, knowing how his team would react, made sure that copies of the article were hanging all around the clubhouse. And when the players arrived, Rick Dempsey, the veteran reserve catcher, expressed the anger that the entire team felt. "Those are some pretty cocky statements from someone who hasn't been in baseball very long. You can tell that his success has gone to his mouth a little bit. But his day will come. He's going to hit the ground. He's going down hard."

Cone not only went down hard, he went down fast, giving up five runs in only two innings. It was the earliest departure of the year for the young right-hander, who in an otherwise sensational season had traveled the road from mediocrity to a 20-3 record. It was obvious that the Dodgers' angry reaction to the column had unnerved Cone and caused him to lose his rhythm. "You could see how upset he was," said Mets catcher, Gary Carter. After the game Cone apologized for his remarks, explaining that he hadn't meant them to be taken seriously. He also decided to stop writing the column, but the damage had already been done. Tim Belcher weathered a 2-run homer and three RBI's by Keith Hernandez, and the Dodgers held on to defeat the Mets 6-3 and even the series. "We needed that game desperately," admitted Lasorda. "Everybody was stunned after that horrendous loss in the first game."

Lasorda's decision to play Mickey Hatcher at first base for the slumping Franklin Stubbs also proved to be a key factor in the win. The energetic Hatcher, who was playing in the first postseason game of his ten-year career, scored two runs and had the big hit in the second inning, a two-out line-drive double that knocked in two runs. The glare of the spotlight was an unaccustomed position for the 33-year-old veteran who was more accustomed to a supporting role as captain of the Stuntmen, the nickname taken on by the L.A. reserves. Hatcher, who is so animated that he always seems to be moving in fast-forward even when he's standing still, didn't let Cone's comments affect his play during the game. "Some of the guys were bringing it up every inning. But when I was out there playing, I didn't think about it. My brain can't handle thinking of two things."

The teams moved to the East Coast for game three, which was played despite the fact that it was a cold and wet day and Shea Stadium resembled a swamp as much as it did a baseball diamond. But Tommy Lasorda was feeling bright and sunny because he had his security blanket, Orel Hershiser, to dispel the gloom of the gray day.

And Orel did his job, leaving the game after seven innings, having allowed only one earned run and with the Dodgers leading, 4-3. But in the bottom of the eighth, after Jay Howell had gone to a 3-2 count on Kevin McReynolds, Davey Johnson complained that Howell had something hidden on his glove. The umpires checked the glove, found pine tar, and ejected Howell. Before the inning was over, the Mets had battered three pitchers for five runs and had taken a commanding 8-4 lead. Davey Johnson, looking to restore David Cone's confidence and give him a tune-up for his next start, brought him in to pitch the ninth, and Cone responded by setting the Dodgers down in order. The Mets had grabbed another game from the jaws of defeat and led the series, two games to one.

The next day National League president A. Bartlett Giamatti announced that he was suspending Howell for three days. Howell was upset, explaining that he wasn't a cheater and had used the pine tar only to get a better grip on the ball in the cold weather, not to make it do tricks. Some people thought the punishment wasn't severe enough, while others, including Keith Hernandez, agreed with Howell.

Kirk Gibson and John Tudor, L.A.'s starting pitcher in game four, decided to show their support for Howell by putting his initials on their sleeves. But what the Dodgers found themselves needing was runs, because Doc Gooden and the Mets had them on the ropes and were close to delivering the knockout blow. Gooden, after surrendering two first-inning runs, had been invincible. And in the fourth, the Mets had ridden back-to-back homers by Strawberry and McReynolds to muscle their way to a 3-2 lead. The Mets tacked on another run in the sixth and took their 4-2 lead into the ninth, three outs away from a commanding three-games-to-one lead.

But Gooden committed a pitching sin by walking the leadoff hitter, and then Mike Scioscia made him pay the price by lining his next pitch into the Mets bullpen for a two-run homer that tied the game 4-4. The fans at Shea were shocked into silence, and Gooden and his teammates were stunned. "He's the last guy you think of hitting a home run," said Davey Johnson, knowing that Scioscia had hit only three the entire season. "I thought it was Doc's game."

The teams battled into the 12th inning, and then Kirk Gibson, who hadn't hit a home run in nearly a month, belted a Roger McDowell pitch out of the park to give the Dodgers a 5-4 lead. "I felt I was long overdue," said Gibson, who had managed only one hit in his previous 16 at-bats in the play-offs. "The team was counting on me."

The Mets tried to bounce back in the bottom of the 12th, loading the bases with one out. But ex-Met Jesse Orosco got Strawberry to pop up, and then Lasorda, like Linus reaching for his blanket, brought in Hershiser, the only L.A. pitcher in the park whom he hadn't yet used in game four. After Hershiser induced McReynolds to hit a harmless bloop to center for the final out, Gibson roared, "They say there's Mets magic. What about L.A. magic?"

And the magic and the momentum carried over to the next game, with Gibson swatting a towering three-run home run that led L.A. to a 7-4 win and a 3-2 lead in games.

The Dodgers, who were only one win away from the NL pennant, seemed as surprised as anyone at their situation. "I think we realize we're not the best team in baseball," said Rick Dempsey. And Tommy Lasorda, who liked the underdog's role and who wasn't above trying a little psychological strategy, added, "The Mets have a ton of talent. They're an awesome ball club. I think, without a doubt, they're the best ball club in the National League."

The only down note for the sky-high Dodgers was the fact that Gibson, while stealing second in the ninth inning, had injured his knee and had had to leave the game. As the teams flew back to L.A., the Dodgers were anxious about Gibson's availability for the sixth game while the Mets were hoping that David Cone could pitch them into a seventh game.

But Cone, who was staked to a 1-0 lead in the top of the first, looked like he was coming unglued in the bottom of the inning. Pitching like the strike zone was alien country, Cone walked Sax and Hatcher. And standing in the batter's box, on a hot streak and looking menacing, was Gibson. But after taking the first pitch for a strike, Gibson surprised everyone by bunting at the next delivery. "He was bunting on his own," said a Dodger coach. "I wish he hadn't. And the pitch was a ball. If he had taken it, Cone might have thrown three more balls and never got out of the inning." But instead, Gibson's attempt to put the runners in scoring position turned into a pop-up that Cone grabbed in front of the mound, and given that reprieve, Cone settled down and allowed only a single fifth-inning run while the Mets added four more, including a two-run homer by McReynolds, to force a decisive seventh game.

But anyone who was looking for high drama in the big game quickly had their hopes dashed. The Dodgers took a 1-0 lead in the first on a single by Sax, a double down the third-base line by Hatcher, and a 400-foot sac fly by Gibson. And they ended all the suspense in the second inning by scoring five more runs with the help of some very shoddy fielding by the Mets' infield. With a 6-0 lead and Hershiser on the mound, it was countdown time in L.A. The Mets had run out of miracles. As Darryl Strawberry had warned before the game, "When you keep playing catch-up, eventually it catches up to you."

Lasorda was thrilled. "When we went into this series, we didn't think we belonged on the same field with the Mets. This is my dream. We beat the best." But even while the Dodgers were celebrating their victory, which had been built on determination, aggressive base-running, timely hitting, and MVP pitching by Hershiser, their critics were still sniping. "With all due respect to the Los Angeles Dodgers," said Whitey Herzog, "the best team in the National League isn't going to be playing the Oakland Athletics in the World Series. Over 162 games, form holds up, but in seven games, chance may show up. And that's what happened to the Mets."

If Lasorda was right and the Dodgers didn't belong on the same field with the Mets, they didn't belong in the same stadium with the powerful Athletics. Oakland had a stronger player at every starting position except left field and second base. And any edge that Hershiser seemed to give L.A.'s pitching staff was apparently offset by the depth of the A's staff. And if facts and figures weren't enough, the A's even had history on their side: The Dodgers were 0-6 in World Series when they hosted the first game, and the A's were 5-1 when they opened on the road.

And then on game day, Lasorda got a piece of news that he absolutely didn't want to hear: Gibson's leg was so severely injured that he couldn't even come out for the pregame introductions. The Dodgers, though, refused to fold and came out fighting. In the bottom of the first, Stewart hit Sax, and two pitches later, Hatcher, who had hit only one home run in 191 at-bats during the season, lashed a two-run homer over the wall in left center.

But the Athletics battled back in the top of the second, loading the bases against Belcher on a single and two walks. And then Canseco made Belcher pay for his wildness by rocketing a grand-slam home run over the center-field fence to give the A's a 4-2 lead. And as Canseco and Mark McGwire celebrated in their usual style by smashing forearms, it seemed that the rightful order of things had been restored to the baseball diamond. And even after L.A. had narrowed the gap to 4-3 with three successive singles in the sixth, they were still a run shy in the ninth. And the A's had Eckersley ready to preserve the order and close out the game.

While Eckersley was taking his warmup tosses, Gibson, who had spent the entire game in the trainer's room with an ice pack on his right knee, was up in the Dodger's clubhouse taking practice swings against a batting tee. "I was very disappointed. I knew I couldn't play. But I thought maybe I could suck it up for one AB and something could happen." As Eckersley completed his tosses, Gibson sent a message to Lasorda, "If you want to go ahead and hit Mike [Davis] for Alfredo [Griffin], I'll hit in the pitcher's spot."

But it didn't look as though Gibson would get

his AB, as Eckersley got Scioscia to pop out and then fanned Jeff Hamilton. And the Dodgers, down to their last out, were down to Mike Davis, who hadn't hit his weight during the season. But suddenly, Eckersley lost his fine edge and walked Davis. "That was terrible. A two-out walk to any hitter is inexcusable. I tried to go right at him. I just kept missing."

While Davis went down to first, Gibson limped out of the dugout, and the crowd at Dodger Stadium saluted his courageous effort with a standing ovation. But it became painfully obvious as Gibson fouled off the first three pitches that he was unable to stride into a pitch and take a full cut. With the count at 2-2, Davis stole second, and when Eckersley missed with the next pitch the scene was set as though it were a Hollywood movie: the hotshot pitcher overpowering the brave but injured slugger in the World Series, with two outs in the last of the ninth and a 3-2 count. Eckersley, who hadn't thrown anything to Gibson except his heater, was thinking fastball again. But catcher Ron Hassey was thinking that Gibson was set up for the slider. "I thought it would freeze him and he wouldn't be able to hit it. If Dennis puts it in the right spot, we get him out."

But Dennis didn't put it in the right spot; he put it out over the plate, down below the belt, in Gibson's power alley. Striding painfully into the pitch, Gibson whipped his bat around and with one hand sent the ball crashing in a long arc deep into the right-field stands. As the fans in Dodger Stadium went wild, and the A's stood in stunned stillness, Gibson punched his fist into the air and took off on a slow but triumphant hobble around the bases.

Gibson became just the seventh player ever to end a World Series game with a home run and the only one to bring his team from behind while doing it. When he came into the clubhouse, there was a cardboard sign hung on his locker with two words that said it all: ROY HOBBS. But that was to be THE NATURAL's last appearance in the 1988 World Series. The Dodgers would have to find the way without the man who had taught them how to win.

Fortunately for the Dodgers, they still had Hershiser to throw at the A's in game two, and he proved to be a lot more than they could handle. Orel was a triple threat, using his arm, his bat, and his legs to subdue the A's, 6-0.

He took care of the pitching by tossing a three-hitter (all singles by Dave Parker), and became the first pitcher to throw shutouts in the LCS and the World Series in the same year. Orel also outstroked Oakland, collecting two doubles and a single, scoring the first run of the game, and knocking in the last while becoming the first pitcher in 64 years to hammer three hits in a World Series game. He scored the only run he would need in the third, when he started a five-run uprising with a single. He went from first to third on a single by Sax, challenging Canseco's strong arm, and then came in to score on a single by Stubbs. While Orel was catching his breath, Hatcher knocked in Sax with a hit-and-run single over second base, and then Mike Marshall put the game out of reach by crashing a Storm Davis fastball into the left-field stands. The game was as good as over, but Orel hadn't finished having fun. One inning later he drove in the sixth and final run with a double, and then added another two-bagger in the sixth.

Orel's teammates were in awe of his accomplishments. "I don't know what he can do next," said Steve Sax. "Maybe he'll just fly out of the stadium. I won't be shocked." But the A's, despite having been shut out and, except for Parker, no-hitted, seemed mystified by Orel's mastery, reacting as though he was some sort of carnival conjurer relying on sleight of hand. "He's not overpowering," said McGwire, who seemed puzzled by the A's inability to hit Hershiser. And Canseco, using humor more effectively than his bat, quipped, "My first impression of Hershiser is he's a heck of a hitter. I'm going to hire him as my personal hitting coach."

The A's, despite being down 2-0, were still confident that they would turn things around against their California cousins. As Tony LaRussa put it, "They haven't put us in a desperate situation." But this certainly wasn't the way it was supposed to be—the Oakland steamroller getting flattened by the lightweights from L.A. Or as Mark McGwire said, sounding just a little like Dorothy in Oz, "It's not where we expected to be, that's for sure."

The A's finally broke through for a run in the third inning of game four, their first score after nineteen innings of futility. But L.A. tied the game in the fifth on an RBI double by Franklin Stubbs.

The teams stayed tied into the ninth, and Lasorda turned the ball over to Jay Howell, who was making his first appearance since the pine-tar incident ten days earlier. Howell got off to a good start by getting Canseco to pop out, but then Mark McGwire, who had been hitless in the World Series, jumped all over a 2-2 fastball and sent it over the left-center-field fence to give the A's a 2-1 win. "You dream about a thing like that," said a grinning McGwire. "I had been thinking how great that must have been for Kirk when he hit his homer, and now I know even more."

The Dodgers, still up two games to one and already flying high, received an extra emotional lift from an unexpected source prior to game four. They were sitting around the clubhouse watching the pregame show on NBC-TV and heard sportscaster Bob Costas say that with Gibson and Mike Marshall, who was forced out of game three with an injury, unavailable, the Dodgers might have the weakest hitting team ever to play in a World Series. It wasn't such an outrageous statement, considering the fact that during the season Canseco had out-homered the entire line-up that L.A. put on the field for game four. But the Dodgers weren't interested in facts. According to Lasorda, "The team went nuts." And the Dodgers' manager couldn't have been happier as he heard his players screaming, "We'll show him."

And L.A., with Sax and Hatcher leading the way, did scratch their way to a 4-2 lead. But then in the bottom of the seventh, the A's, seeing the World Series slipping through their grasp, went on the attack. Walt Weiss broke an 0-12 slump with a one-out single, and one out later Henderson doubled him home to cut L.A.'s lead to 4-3. And then Lasorda made a move that really had the Oakland fans cheering—he signaled for Jay Howell. "I told him that I was going to get him back in a game as quick as I could."

But despite his manager's vote of confidence, Howell, who was surprised to be back on the mound so quickly, got off to a shaky start by walking Canseco. And after Alfredo Griffin prolonged the inning by muffing Dave Parker's line drive, the A's had the bases loaded and Mark McGwire at the plate. Howell's first pitch to the big first baseman was an inside fastball, the same pitch that McGwire had hit out of the park to win game three. But this time McGwire popped it up, and the inning and the threat were over. "It was a matter of millimeters. One millimeter down, I drive it. One millimeter up, I pop it up. You see the ball, you drive it, or maybe you swing under it, like tonight. The ball is pitched, and you hit it. Or maybe you don't. It's the game of baseball."

The A's had another shot in the ninth inning when with one out Henderson singled for his fourth hit of the game and Canseco, the majors' leading home-run hitter, came up, representing the winning run. With the count at 2-1, and the A's fans screaming for Jose to pop one, Howell threw him a hanging curve ball. "He gave me a pitch I should have hit out. I saw it and my eyes opened up." But all he did was foul it back. And with the count at 3-2, Howell threw a slider for strike three. "That was a nasty pitch," said Canseco. "It looked like the bottom fell out of it." Then Howell got Parker to pop up to third for the last out, giving the Dodgers an exciting win and a commanding 3-1 lead.

While Howell was celebrating "the biggest win of my life," Lasorda was tossing zingers at Costas. "What a tremendous victory for one of the weakest teams in the history of the World Series to beat one of the strongest teams. They're so good, they should spot us some runs before the game begins."

There was no humor coming out of the Athletics' clubhouse, though, only confusion and frustration. "We don't know all year what losing means," said Luis Polonia. "Look where we are now. We see our team; we see theirs. We didn't think it would be that tough."

And Canseco, who hadn't had a hit since his grand slam in game one, echoed his teammate. "This is a shock. I couldn't tell you what's going on right now. This is a tough thing to swallow." And life wasn't going to get any easier for the A's, because coming up against them in game five was Orel Hershiser.

Mickey Hatcher, who had been keying L.A.'s offense since Lasorda had inserted him into the starting lineup in game two of the NLCS, jump-started the Dodgers' attack in the first inning as he had in game one by lining a two-run homer over the left-field wall. Hatcher, going around the bases like Roadrunner, nearly passed Franklin Stubbs. "I still haven't learned how to do a home-run trot," said Hatcher, which was not surprising since he had hit only 35 in his entire career. Mickey was so excited that he started bashing forearms and almost put himself on the disabled list. "I won't do that again. I almost broke my arm."

The A's finally nicked Hershiser for a run in the third inning, but in the top of the fourth Hatcher got things going again by beating out an infield roller with a head-first dive into first. After Storm Davis fanned Marshall and Shelby, Mike Davis, the forgotten Dodger, who was playing only because of Marshall's injury, was given the green light on a 3-0 pitch and hit a tremendous blast deep into the right-field seats. It was a magic moment in an otherwise disappointing season for Davis. He had been signed as a high-priced free agent and was supposed to become the Dodgers' regular right fielder. But by June he had become a regular benchwarmer, and finished the season with a .196 batting average, two homers and 17 RBI's in 108 at bats. But Davis didn't sulk or go into a funk. He kept working out, kept taking his practice cuts so that he would be ready to help out when his opportunity came. And as Davis slowly circled the bases—"I wanted it to last forever"—he savored a season's worth of sweetness and satisfaction.

While the Dodgers were flexing their seldom-used home-run muscles and stretching their lead to 5-1 with a sixth-inning run, Hershiser was humming along, holding Oakland hitless between the fourth and seventh innings. But then, in the eighth inning, he momentarily lost his rhythm and his control, and the A's pushed across a second run. "I really thought he was losing it," said Lasorda. "I had the bullpen up and ready." Canseco, representing the tying run, battled Hershiser to a full count, and then Orel ran a fastball in on Jose's fists and got him to pop up weakly to first base. Then he fanned dangerous Dave Parker to end the threat.

Orel made quick work of the A's in the ninth, ending the inning, the game, and the World Series with a flourish by striking out Tony Phillips. The Dodgers, who had dared to dream the impossible dream, had become the world champions.

Hershiser, who allowed only two runs in his two World Series wins, was named the MVP. And Kirk Gibson wasn't exaggerating when he paid tribute to his teammate by saying, "For as long as we live, we may never see a pitcher accomplish what he's accomplished." But Hershiser, realizing that this wasn't a time for individual awards, held up the trophy and yelled, "Hey guys, this is for you."

And Lasorda, knowing that the World Series victory had as much to do with players like Hatcher and Davis as it did with Gibson and Hershiser, summed up the Dodgers remarkable achievement. "This is, without a doubt, the greatest accomplishment of a team that didn't have the greatest talent. But we had guys who had that desire. Nobody believed we could win our division; nobody believed we could beat the Mets and the A's. It's David and Goliath. This is an example for everybody in the world of what you can do if you want something bad enough. I've said it all along; this is a team of destiny."

CHAPTER 7

Swept Away

In the annual game of musical chairs, there were three new teams at the top of their divisions and, after an eleven-year wait, one repeat winner.

In the National League West, the San Francisco Giants, who were picked to be a fourth-place finisher by most so-called experts, rode the arms of a pitching staff stitched together by managerial wizard Roger Craig and the red-hot bats of Will Clark and Kevin Mitchell, who led the major leagues in home runs and RBI's, to their second divisional title in three years.

And in the NL East, the lowly Cubs woke from a five-year hibernation and roared into first place past the feuding Mets and the crippled Cardinals. The Cubs combined the talents of the league's top rookies, out-fielders Jerome Walton and Dwight Smith, with those of all-stars Ryne Sandberg, Shawon Dunston, and Mark Grace, and added some surprise pitching performances to create their winning recipe. The Cubs' winning charge had caught a lot of experts off-guard, including Steve Wulf, who had written in *Sports Illustrated* in the spring that "the Cubs, who haven't won a world championship since 1908, have had only one winning season since 1972. You can be certain this will not be their second." But the Cubs, with manager Don Zimmer pushing all the right buttons, had defied all expectations and taken the title. "Maybe we've only got the fifth-best talent in the division," said first baseman Mark Grace, "but we've got it here," he said, pointing to his heart.

In the American League, the Toronto Blue Jays, the team that always seems to have great talent but who doesn't win many trophies, beat back a down-to-the-wire challenge from the Baltimore Orioles to win the Eastern Division. The Jays, who had often folded in the stretch in previous years, were thrilled. "It's as if the curse has been lifted," said their ace reliever, Tom Henke, after he closed out the division-winning game.

The Oakland Athletics spotted the A.L. West long-term injuries to Jose Canseco, the League's MVP in 1988; Dennis Eckersley, the top reliever in the league; and Walt Weiss, the 1988 Rookie of the Year, and still managed to compile the best record in the major leagues for the second consecutive year. The A's were able to withstand the injuries because of the addition of two key players: right-hander Mike Moore, who earned 19 victories, two behind teammate Dave Stewart, who had bagged a league-leading 21 wins; and left-fielder Rickey Henderson, whom the A's had brought home to Oakland in a mid-season trade with the New York Yankees. Henderson, with his .411 on-base percentage and his major-league-best 77 stolen bases, had ignited the A's attack. As Oakland's manager, Tony LaRussa, noted, "He gave our offense a boost when we needed it the most. Rickey's a rare package of speed and power who can disrupt a game like no one else."

The A's had also added a new and more determined attitude after their surprising and embarrassing loss to the Dodgers in the 1988 World Series. In 1989, they were a team on a mission to win the series and establish themselves as the best team in all of baseball.

Will Clark led the Giants into Chicago for game one of the National League Championship Series and immediately began showing the fans in Wrigley Field why he's known as Will the Thrill. He opened the scoring with a first-inning RBI double that ignited a three-run rally. And after Grace had closed the gap with a two-run homer, Clark stretched it out again with a solo blast in the third inning. Sandberg gave the Cubs another flicker of hope with a four-bagger into the left-field seats in the bottom of the inning. But then, in the top of the fourth, Clark put out that light when, with the bases loaded, he hit a screaming line drive out of Wrigley Field to give the Giants an 8–3 lead. And then Kevin Mitchell made it seem that much darker for the Cubs when he poled a three-run homer in the eighth inning. But it was Clark's blast that had done the damage. "Not only did he hit a grand slam, he hit it into the street. That pretty much demoralized us," said Mark Grace.

The Cubs played payback in the second game as they rocked the Giants' ace, "Big Daddy" Rick Reuschel, for six first-inning runs. Even Mike Bielecki, the Cubs' starting pitcher, who had hit an anemic .043 during the season, chipped in with a two-run single. And Mark Grace, whose three-for-four performance in game one had been dwarfed by the giant shadow cast by Will Clark, lashed an RBI double in the first inning and then put the game out of reach with a bases-clearing three-run double that powered the Cubs to a 9–5 win.

The series shifted to San Francisco's Candlestick Park for game three, but the Giants proved to be rude hosts, pulling out a late-inning thriller when Robby Thompson lashed a two-run homer off Les Lancaster in the bottom of the eighth to give the Giants a 5–4 win and a 2–1 lead in games.

Will Clark and Mark Grace continued their torrid hitting in game four, but it was the Giants' rookie third baseman, Matt Williams, who stole the show. He stroked a two-out, two-run single in the third to give the Giants a 3–2 lead. And then in the fifth inning, Williams closed out the scoring by crashing a two-run homer off Steve Wilson that gave the Giants the 6–4 win and put them only one victory away from their first World Series appearance in 27 years.

Game five turned on two late-inning matchups, and the Giants came out on top both times. In the first one, the Cubs' bullpen ace, Mitch Williams, who is known as "The Wild Thing," was called in to pitch to William Clark in the eighth inning of a 1–1 tie. It was a classic confrontation. The Wild Thing vs. Will the Thrill. Lights. Camera. Action. Clark, who had already singled and tripled and scored the Giants' only run of the game, fought off two one-and-two fastballs. "I fouled off a couple of tough pitches from a tough pitcher. My heart was racing just a little." Williams came right back with the heater on his next pitch, but this time Clark got the fat part of the bat on the ball and smashed it into center field, sending the winning runs streaking across the plate.

But the Cubs did not go gently down to defeat. They ignited a two-out ninth-inning rally that narrowed the score to 3–2 with two men on base before the Giants' closer, Steve Bedrosian, retired their best clutch hitter, Ryne Sandberg, and put an end to their season.

Clark, who had an awesome series that included a .650 batting average and eight RBI's, was named the NLCS MVP. And Mark Grace, who had quite a series himself, notching a .647 average and eight RBI's, showed a lot of class in defeat. "No regrets, no excuses. We played as hard as we possibly could. All five games were battles. It was the most fun I've ever had."

And over in the American League Rickey Henderson, who had always dreamed of playing in the

World Series, took his game to another level against the Blue Jays and made sure that his dream became the A's reality.

Rickey made the key play in game one when he took out Toronto's second baseman, Nelson Liriano, on an attempted double play in the sixth inning with the score tied 3–3. Rickey's hard slide caused Liriano's throw to first to sail wide and allowed the winning runs to cross the plate. Rickey had set the tone of the American League Championship Series in his first at-bat in the opening inning when he drew a walk and promptly stole second. And he put the exclamation point on the A's 7–3 lead in the eighth inning when he walked, stole second, took third on a wild pitch, and then trotted home on Carney Lansford's single.

And it was the Rickey Henderson Show all over again in game two, as the fleet left-fielder went two-for-two, swiped *four* bases (which gave him a play-off record six for the series), scored two runs, and led the A's to a 6–3 win while totally demoralizing the Blue Jays.

After the game, Toronto's third baseman, Kelly Gruber, and catcher, Ernie Whitt, were furious at what they considered to be the "hot dog" antics of Rickey and designated hitter Dave Parker. Gruber took exception to Parker's slow-motion trot around the bases after the A's slugger had belted a sixth-inning home run. And Whitt was bent out of shape because Rickey had slowed down and not even bothered to slide on his seventh-inning steal of second (despite the fact that Whitt had conceded the base to Rickey by not even throwing down to second).

But Mookie Wilson, the ex-Met who had fueled Toronto's drive to the division title, thought his teammates ought to concentrate on *their* game. "It's okay to have some fun out there when you're winning. That kind of stuff shouldn't be our concern." And Toronto manager Cito Gaston even found some humor in the predicament that Henderson presented to his team. "Probably we should throw to third when Rickey's stealing second, and maybe we can at least beat him to third."

The playoffs moved to Toronto's SkyDome for game three, and the Blue Jays finally pulled out a win, 7–3. The hometown Toronto fans got the opportunity to hoot at Henderson and Parker, but the two stars held their own. Parker answered their taunts with a fourth-inning home run, and Rickey doubled, stole a base, and scored two runs before the Jays finally got him out on his third trip to the plate. Afterward, Rickey was playful in talking about the fans. "I know they're going to hooray me; that's okay. I'd rather have a house full of noisy fans than an empty stadium." Rickey, though, wasn't as tolerant toward the Toronto team. "In a way I'm glad they won. Now they can stop cryin' and come out and play baseball."

But then he turned mellow again when he was asked about the fans in left field who had pelted him with hot dogs. "I was looking to see if any had mustard on them." And finally Rickey turned serious. "If they think my stealing is hot-dogging, I'll tell you what I'll do. Tomorrow I won't run. I'll just hit a couple of home runs."

And Rickey went out and immediately began delivering on his boast in the third inning of game four by crushing a two-run, 440-foot homer to straightaway center. Rickey jived his way around the bases and then punctuated his performance with a long round of forearm bashing with his teammates.

One out later Jose Canseco got in on the act in a big way by hitting a humungous home run into the fifth deck of the SkyDome. As Jose stood at the plate and admired his moon shot, Dave Parker just gasped, "Oh my god! You just saw something you can tell your grandchildren about."

And then Rickey finished living up to his own challenge by hammering another two-run homer, this one off the left-field foul pole, as the A's went on to win 6–5.

And Rickey kept the pressure on in game five by drawing a leadoff walk, stealing second, and then cruising home on a Canseco single. In the third inning Rickey played long ball, whacking an RBI triple to center that upped the A's lead to 2–0. Oakland added two more runs in the eighth, and then, when Dave Stewart, who had shut the Jays out for seven innings, began to run out of gas, LaRussa called in Eckersley. Dennis, who saved three of the A's four wins, put out the fire and preserved the 4–3 win that made the A's the first repeat pennant winners since the New York Yankees, who turned the trick in 1977–78.

Rickey Henderson, who played a decisive role in each of the A's four wins, was a unanimous choice as the ALCS Most Valuable Player. Rickey, putting on one of the best postseason performances of all times, led both teams with nine runs scored, five RBI's, and a postseason-record eight stolen bases. He also smashed two home runs and batted .400 while reaching base in fourteen of 23 plate appearances. As Dave Parker said, "I've been in a few of these things, and I've never seen anyone bring it up to a level like he did. This was the Rickey Henderson Show."

San Francisco and Oakland are like Siamese cities: separated by the San Francisco Bay but connected by the San Francisco–Oakland Bay Bridge. So there was a lot of excitement in the area for the World Series, which was being billed as "The Battle of the Bay."

But the first game, played in Oakland Coliseum, was more a blowout than a battle. The A's struck for five early runs that included solo home runs by Dave Parker, his first in 45 World Series at-bats, and the light-hitting Walt Weiss, who had hit only three round-trippers all season.

And those five runs were more than enough offense, because Dave Stewart wasn't giving the Giants *any* runs. The A's ace made it look easy as he tossed his first shutout of the season while cutting the Giants down to size. Roger Craig, the Giants' manager, summed up the game very simply. "He had a real good, live fastball, and we just couldn't make contact."

And in game two the Giants must have thought they were seeing double as they fell to Mike Moore, 5–1. Rickey Henderson got the A's rolling in the first when he worked Rick Reuschel for a walk, stole second, and then motored home on an opposite-field double by Carney Lansford. After the Giants tied the score in the third, the A's erupted for four fourth-inning runs that iced the game and put the Giants a step closer to the deep freeze. Canseco got the rally going by coaxing a walk out of Reuschel and then raced home with the second run when Parker rapped a line-drive double off the right-field wall. After surrendering a base on balls to Dave Henderson, Reuschel looked as though he might escape further damage when he fanned Mark McGwire. But catcher Terry Steinbach belted a three-run homer deep to left that put the game out of reach, because Moore, relying on a wicked split-fingered fastball that had the Giant batters chasing balls in the dirt, coasted along on a three-hitter through the first seven innings. And when he gave up a leadoff single in the eighth, LaRussa went to his bullpen, and Rick Honeycutt and Dennis Eckersley took turns setting the Giants down in order to preserve the victory.

The A's, up two games to none and making it look ridiculously easy, weren't mouthing off, but their confidence came oozing out. "If things are going right, it's very hard for another team to beat us," offered Rickey Henderson. And then Tony LaRussa gave the Giants a message they didn't want to hear: "I think we've been playing good. But I know we can play better."

Meanwhile, over in the Giants' clubhouse, Kevin Mitchell was complaining about his team's lackluster play. "It's just not as exciting as it was against the Cubs. It seems like everybody's dead now. They get the big play, and we just shut down." And manager Roger Craig, seeing his team bogged down in a collective slump, decided to shake up his lineup for game three.

But, at 5:04 P.M., thirty minutes before game three was scheduled to begin in Candlestick Park, Mother Nature did some shaking of her own. "I heard Dusty Baker [the Giants' batting coach] yell 'Earthquake!' " said catcher Terry Kennedy. "I thought he was kidding and just trying to keep things loose. But I knew something was wrong when I saw the first-base dugout moving."

The quake didn't cause much damage to Candlestick Park, and more importantly, there were no injuries. But the toll of lives and property around the Bay Area was severe. Out of respect for the loss of life and homes, and in order to give the Bay Area time to recuperate, baseball Commissioner Fay Vincent postponed game three of the 1989 World Series.

And the situation was so serious that twelve days passed before the two teams squared off against each other. The teams had done their best to stay sharp during the long delay, with the A's even spending some time at their spring-training headquarters in Phoenix. But as Tony LaRussa pointed out, "It's not easy to keep telling yourself to stay ready." Most baseball people figured that the long layoff would hurt the pitchers more than the hitters, and that the Giants would benefit more than the A's. As California Angels manager Doug Rader pointed out, "It's fair to assume that San Francisco's offense isn't going to get any worse."

And, in fact, the Giants' offense did spring to life, but the A's, led by the "other" Henderson, centerfielder Dave, had too much firepower for their outgunned "cousins" from across the Bay. Carney Lansford got things going in the first inning with a one-out single. That brought up Jose Canseco, who hadn't had a World Series hit since the first game of the *1988* Series. Jose was also feeling a bit out of it because of the quake and all the time off, but Scott Garrelts got Jose's attention real quick by throwing two pitches right under his chin. Jose made some menacing moves toward Garrelts, but kept his cool and answered the brush back pitches by snapping out of his 0–23 World Series slump with a sharp single to left. One out later Dave Henderson drove in both runners with a double off the wall in right field that was just a few inches shy of clearing the fence.

The Giants cut the lead in half in the bottom of the second when Matt Williams broke an 0-for-8 slump with a solo homer off Dave Stewart. Two innings later, though, the A's stretched their lead to 4–1 as Dave Henderson and Tony Phillips poked home runs. But the Giants bounced back in the bottom of the fourth as Terry Kennedy delivered a clutch two-out single that knocked in Clark and Mitchell and cut the A's lead to 4–3. And the A's were spared further damage only because Mark McGwire made a superb diving stop of a hot smash by Pat Sheridan to end the inning. A grateful Dave Stewart later called it "the play of the game."

In the fifth inning the A's gave their ace some breathing room when Jose Canseco walloped a three-run homer that upped their lead to 7–3. "That was the ballgame," said Rickey Henderson. "See, they woke him up. You do that with Jose, and he'll do something great. He *crushed* that ball." One out later Dave Henderson did some crushing of his own, lining a fastball over the fence in left center; and one inning later Carney Lansford got into the act by stroking another four-bagger, which upped the A's lead to 9–3. In the eighth the A's played pile-on, and added four more runs. The Giants scored four meaningless runs in the ninth off Gene Nelson that narrowed the final score to 13–7, but it was much too little and way too late.

Dave Stewart, who became the only pitcher ever to win two playoff and two World Series games in the same season, had given the A's a big boost with seven solid innings. "We didn't know how anybody would be after all that time off, but Stew was ready. He threw some pretty wicked pitches," said Terry Steinbach, the man who was catching those pitches. "It was as if he were taking his regular turn in the rotation," marveled the A's pitching coach, Dave Duncan.

The Giants were still talking tough. "We can still win four in a row," said Will Clark. But he was just whistling in the dark. The A's had beaten the Giants eight-of-nine in spring training and three in a row in October, and they weren't about to suffer a loss of confidence now. When Rickey Henderson was asked if there was any way the A's would lose, he seemed amused. "Not unless our bus gets lost in traffic. Or all our pitchers get hurt."

Then Rickey went out and opened game four by losing Don Robinson's third pitch over the wall, to give the A's a 1-0 lead. Rickey hit it so high and so far that some people thought he was working for NASA. The game really began to slip away from the Giants in the second inning, when pitcher Mike Moore lashed a two-out, two-run double over Brett Butler's head in straightaway center and then came home to score on a single by Rickey Henderson, boosting the A's lead to 4-0. It was Moore's first Major League hit and broke an 0-70 string of hitless World Series appearances for American League pitchers. The Giants were beginning to have that "We've been here before" look.

The A's stretched that lead to 8-0 before the silent Giant bats woke up in the bottom of the sixth, and Kevin Mitchell hit a two-run homer. And then, an inning later, the fans in Candlestick finally had a chance to roar as the Giants cut the lead to 8–6 and had a man on base with Will Clark and Kevin Mitchell coming up. But Rick Honeycutt got Clark on a short fly before Mitchell teed off against Todd Burns, sending Rickey racing back to the fence to haul down the towering fly for the third out of the inning.

The tide still could have turned in the Giants' direction, but they gave the A's a gift run in the eighth on three straight walks after Lansford legged out an infield roller. "It changed the momentum back to our side," noted Dave Henderson. And the A's made sure that it stayed that way, as Burns set the Giants down in order in the eighth. And then Eckersley, with the help of two defensive gems by Tony Phillips, closed out the game that made the Oakland Athletics the champions of the world.

It was a moment of great joy and quiet satisfaction for the A's, who had dedicated themselves to winning the World Series. "This year we weren't going to be denied," said Dave Parker. "When we got back to this point, these ballplayers turned into meat-eating tigers."

In the clubhouse the A's celebrated happily with their families. But, out of respect for the victims of the earthquake, the party was low key, and there was no champagne. When Dave Stewart was presented with the trophy as Series MVP, he took that opportunity to demonstrate that the real greatness of the A's lay in the fact that they were a *team* rather than a collection of individual stars. Stewart held the trophy high above his head and told Rickey Henderson that it was his to share. "Rickey definitely had MVP numbers. Dave Henderson, Mike Moore, Terry Steinbach, Carney Lansford, they all had an MVP series.

"I wasn't too shabby. But being the number-one team in the world—that's the big prize. And we all share that, all twenty-four guys on the team, and the coaches, and the manager."

The A's, who became the first team to sweep a World Series since the Cincinnati Reds swept the Yankees in 1976, had thoroughly dominated the Giants. They outscored them 32–14, outhit them .301 to .209, outpitched them, and never trailed in any of the games. "It was like going up against a tidal wave," said Terry Kennedy. "After a while you get swept away."

You might enjoy keeping score of the next World Series. You can do this by simply filling in what is called a line score, or you can get more involved by keeping track of every play.

This is a line score. If you decide to use this type of scorecard, draw it on a separate piece of paper.

To keep a line score, put the names of the teams in the empty boxes on the left-hand side (the visiting team goes on top because they bat first; that is why the first half of each inning is called the "top" half and the last half of each inning is called the "bottom" half). After each half-inning, put in the number of runs that the team scored, or a zero if they didn't score. At the end of the game, put each team's total runs under the *R* column. You can also keep track of each team's hits and errors on the side or on another piece of paper and then put those totals in at the end of the game under the *H* and *E* columns.

	1	2	3	4	5	6	7	8	9	10	R	H	E
Name of Team 1													
Name of Team 2													

This is a more involved scorecard. Use one sheet for each team. These forms appear at the back of the book.

Name of Team		1	2		INNING 1
4 2nd Baseman		z-4			4 singled, thrown out stealing (catcher to second baseman).
SUBSTITUTE PLAYER					
8 Center Fielder		FC = (PB)			8 doubled, advanced to 3rd on a fielder's choice, scored on passed ball.
SUBSTITUTE PLAYER					
5 3rd Baseman		13			5 thrown out (pitcher to 1st)
SUBSTITUTE PLAYER					
DH Designated Hitter		HP			DH Hit by pitch. Took 1st base.
SUBSTITUTE PLAYER					
3 1st Baseman		7			3 flied out to left field.
SUBSTITUTE PLAYER					

				INNING 2
2 Catcher			6-4	2 walked, later forced out shortstop to 2nd base (1st half of double play).
SUBSTITUTE PLAYER			SB	
7 Left Fielder			DP	7 hit into double play (shortstop to 2nd base to 1st base).
SUBSTITUTE PLAYER			6-4-3	
9 Right Fielder			(≡)	9 hit home run.
SUBSTITUTE PLAYER				
6 Shortstop				6 fouled out to 1st base.
SUBSTITUTE PLAYER			3F	
1 Pitcher				
SUBSTITUTE PLAYER				
TOTALS	R / H	1 / 2	1 / 1	

To use the scorecard, fill in the team name for the visiting team in the top left and then fill in the starting line-up in the empty spaces under the team name. Then write in the name of the home team and fill in its starting line-up. Space has also been provided so that you can fill in the names of all the players (you can probably get the roster from your local newspaper). This way you will be able to see who the manager can call on to pinch-hit or bring on in relief.

To keep score, you will need to know the code that is used. It is based on numbering players by position. Number the players as follows:

1 – Pitcher	4 – Second Baseman	7 – Left Fielder
2 – Catcher	5 – Third Baseman	8 – Center Fielder
3 – First Baseman	6 – Shortstop	9 – Right Fielder
	DH – Designated Hitter	

Symbols for plays:

Single –	Hit by Pitcher–HP
Double =	Wild Pitch–WP
Triple ≡	Called Out On Strikes–KC
Home Run ≡	Bunt–B
Sacrifice–SH	Win–W
Walk–BB	Passed Ball–PB
Intentional Walk–IW	Stolen Base–SB
Line Drive–L	Force Out–FO
Strikeout–K	Double Play–DP
Balk–BK	Error–E
Foul Fly–F	Sacrifice Fly–SF
Fielder's Choice–FC	Change of Pitcher or Batter–∿∿
AB — the *total* number of at-bats that the player had during the game	R — *total* runs
	E — *total* errors that the *individual* player was charged with during the game
H — *total* hits	

Every time a batter goes to the plate, use the number to show either how he was retired or reached base. Fielding plays that retire batters or runners also call for the use of numbers. For example, if a batter is retired on a grounder to the third baseman, it is recorded as *5 − 3,* because the third baseman (number *5*) threw it to the first baseman (number *3*). If the batter flies out to the left fielder, then you put a 7 (because the left fielder is number 7). If the batter fouled out to the left fielder, then you write *7F.*

Here's an example of how a play would be scored in a box on the scorecard:

In the example above, the batter reached first on an error by the shortstop, stole second, went to third on a passed ball, and scored on a wild pitch. *WP* is circled to indicate that a run was scored on the play.

Now that you've read this book, you should be all set to keep score. Following are enough scorecards for you to use throughout the World Series games. (If necessary, you can photocopy them to make more.) Need practice? Begin by keeping score of a play-off game first. Just remember: don't get so caught up in keeping records that you forget to enjoy the game!

	1	2	3	4	5	6	7	8	9	10	AB	R	H	RBI	E
TOTALS															

	1	2	3	4	5	6	7	8	9	10	AB	R	H	RBI	E
TOTALS															

I hope that you liked this book. If you did,
you would probably like our other sports titles
by Richard J. Brenner:

Michael Jordan • Magic Johnson. A dual
biography of the two most popular athletes
in America. A look behind the scenes and
above the rim.

 • Featuring 12 exciting photos.

Joe Montana • Jerry Rice. A double biography
of the two San Francisco 49er football superstars.
From childhood dreams to Super Bowl wins.

 • Featuring 12 pages of exciting photos.

The Complete Super Bowl Story Games I-XXIV.
The most exciting moments in Super Bowl history
are brought to life, game-by-game.

 • Featuring 16 pages of action-packed photos.
 • Record Sheets for Super Bowl XXV.